BLACK AUTHENTICITY

BLACK AUTHENTICITY

A Psychology for Liberating People of African Descent

Marcia Sutherland, Ph.D.

Copyright 1993 by Marcia Sutherland

All rights reserved. No part of this book may be reproduced, stored in a retrieval system, or transmitted in any form by any means, electronic, mechanical, photocopying, recording, or otherwise without prior written permission of the author.

Printed in the United States of America

First Printing 1997

04 03 02 01 00 99 98 97   5 4 3 2 1

Cover Design by Niki Mitchell

Library of Congress Cataloging-in-Publication Data

Sutherland, Marcia, 1954-
    Black authenticity: a psychology for liberating people of African descent/ Marcia Sutherland.
      p. cm.
Includes bibliographical references and index.
ISBN: 0-88378-184-0 (cloth)
        0-88378-181-6 (pbk.)
1.Afro-Americans--Psychology. 2.Afro-Americans--Civil rights. 3.Afro-Americans--History. 4.Racism--United States--Psychological aspects. I. Title.
E185.625.S88   1997
155.8'496073--dc21   97-9110
                                                                                CIP

THIRD WORLD PRESS
P.O. Box 19730
Chicago, IL 60619

DEDICATION

To Alice Sutherland, my mother; Grace and Marie, my sisters; Junior, my brother; Kalonji, my son; and all people of African descent: the ancestors, those alive, and those yet to be born. This book is gratefully dedicated to you.

CONTENTS

Dedication v

Foreword ix
    by Dr. A. J. Williams-Myers

Acknowledgments xvii

Chapter I 1
    Psychohistorical Underpinnings
    of White Supremacy

Chapter II 35
    The Role of the Individual in the
    Liberation Struggle

Chapter III 65
    The Marginalization of the African
    World

Chapter IV 91
    Anti-African Practices and Diasporan
    Africans

Chapter V 123
    Reclaiming African Cultural Traditions
    for the Liberation of People of African
    Descent

References 157

Index 195

Foreword

In 1934 Carter G. Woodson published the book *The Miseducation of the Negro*. In that book he spoke of the lack of a cultural identity for the African-American as a result of an education system devoid of positive Black historical contributions. This lack of a cultural identity was the direct result of a Eurocentric school curriculum which overemphasized the contributions of Whites at the expense of people of African descent. For Carter G. Woodson such a curriculum was counterproductive to the socioeconomic and psychological development of Black people. It left them mentally crippled. He wrote:

> ...The Negro's mind has been brought under the control of his oppressor...When you control a man's thinking you do not have to worry about his actions. You do not have to tell him not to stand or go yonder. He will find his 'proper place' and will stay in it. You do not need to send him to the back door. He will go without being told. In fact, if there is no back door, he will cut one for his special benefit...(Woodson, 1934)

Haki R. Madhubuti, in a statement from an unidentified source, and in a similar frame of reference as that of Dr. Woodson, cautions Black educators about an all-White approach to the education of Black youth. He states:

> Our position on Black education is very clear and simple. Either a people prepare their youth to be responsible and responsive to their own needs as a people or somebody else will teach them to be responsible and responsive to somebody else's needs at the expense and detriment to themselves and their people.

Mirroring both Madhubuti and Woodson, the Kenyan writer, Ngugi Wa Thiong'o states that this all-pervasive problem for colonized people is the result of the "cultural bomb" used by imperialists around the world. In his words:

> The effect of a cultural bomb is to annihilate a people's belief in their names, in their languages, in their environment, in their heritage of struggle, in their unity, in their capacities and ultimately in themselves. It makes them see their past as one wasteland of nonachievement and it makes them want to distance themselves from that wasteland. It makes them want to identify with that which is furthest removed from themselves...

Implicit in the words of these authors is the notion of control through a socialization process that, at the fringe of the Black psyche, subliminally implants negative self images that can trigger acts of aggression against other Blacks. Because the socialization process overemphasizes positive images of Whites, there is the tendency for Blacks to mimic White aggressive behavior towards fellow Blacks as a means of releasing penned-up tensions and anxieties brought on by a sense of helplessness in a society where race determines one's life chances. Unable to understand and appreciate their own Africanness, people of African descent find themselves unable to unite in the face of worldwide White oppression.

How was it possible that the African World has reached this state of affairs? Well, to respond to this in a very detailed way would take a book, and these few pages are for the purpose of introducing a book whose thesis addresses this very question. But let me, in my own fashion, succinctly respond.

Culture and language are intertwined. Language is the repository of culture; it is through language that culture is stored, recalled, and expressed. To lose one's language is tantamount to the loss of culture. In parts of the world to which people of African descent were scattered during the transatlantic trade in

Foreword

captives, many African ethnic groups lost their language to that of their oppressors. This weakened the ability of Africans to retain much of their African culture. This was particularly true in North America where the number of African captives imported were relatively small, where the international trade in captives was outlawed much earlier than elsewhere in the Americas, and where the system of cultural genocide was all-pervasive in a society built on the institution of slavery.

In colonial Africa, attempts at deculturalization were supported by the use of the colonizer's language over that of indigenous languages, both in administrative matters and the system of education. Wa Thiong'o's book, *Decolonizing the Mind*, speaks of the importance of language and of the need to return to it as a guarantee against continued cultural erosion.

The call for the rediscovery and the resumption of our language is a call for a regenerative reconnection with the millions of revolutionary tongues in Africa and the world over which are demanding liberation. It is a call for the rediscovery of the real language of humankind. The language of struggle.

Fred Lee Hord, in his book, *Reconstructing Memory*, presents a position similar to Wa Thiong'o regarding the importance of language and culture, and of the need to guard against their lost and/or to "rediscover" (for Africans in North America) the use of culture to combat dehumanization. "If the politics of institutional domination is the necessary strategem for cultural repression," Hord writes, "then the culture of the colonized must provide some political clues to their successful resistance against the repression." Or, as rephrased by Dr. Hord, "...(Black) American scholars have also postulated the centrality of cultural repression in the African-American experience of colonialism. This means that the colonized must understand that centrality in order to enlist culture in their resistance."

People of African descent in North America have experienced cultural erosion and language loss as a result of centuries of White domination. In order to change their peculiar position, they must recapture their African heritage through the reconstruction of their historical memory. Successfully disseminating a reconstructed memory across the school curriculum would lay the seeds for building a collective stand against White oppression.

In Brazil, a country where over 50 percent of the population are people of African descent, "reconstructing memory" to lay the seeds for African unity is a resort to a historical legacy of resistance through the metaphor of quilombo—people collectively united against White oppression as epitomized in an ongoing process of cultural genocide and human degradation. A similar metaphorical stand for those of African descent in Spanish-speaking countries would be palengue.

The Black Consciousness Movement in South Africa was a move to strengthen the collective approach to combating spiritual and physical oblivion. It was, in a sense, reconstructing memory: understanding and appreciating self. According to Gail M. Gerhart, in her book *Black Power in South Africa*, "the Black Consciousness Movement really reiterated the 1940s philosophy of 'Africanism,' and that its aim as an ideology was not to trigger a spontaneous Fanonesque eruption of the masses into violent action, but rather to rebuild and recondition the mind of the oppressed in such a way that eventually they would be ready forcefully to demand what was rightfully theirs."

The above, though succinct, is the state of affairs in the African World today. It is the end result of a trauma induced by colonization and the debate surrounding the liberation strategies necessary to defuse imperialism's "cultural bomb." This brings us to the work of Dr. Marcia Sutherland. Her book is timely, necessary, and so analytically perceptive that it will earn a place for itself on the shelf among the great ones. This book is in the vein of Frantz Fanon's *Black Skin, White Masks*. Sutherland proceeds in a Fanonian fashion to broaden the scope of the debate through suggested ways to reach the collective necessary to defuse the cultural bomb. Fanon spoke to the heart of the problem for the African World, and to which Dr. Sutherland directs her attention in the text, when he wrote:

Foreword

> Every colonized people...in other words, every people in whose soul an inferiority complex has been created by the death and burial of its local cultural originality...finds itself face to face with the language of the civilizing nation; that is, with the culture of the mother country. The colonized is elevated above his jungle status in proportion to his adoption of the mother country's cultural standards. He becomes Whiter as he renounces his blackness, his jungle.

Dr. Sutherland directs her attention not only to the repression of one's culture by the colonizer and the renouncing of one's "blackness, his jungle," but she takes on the all-pervasive issue of the violent nature of White oppression and the need for people of African descent to stand collectively against spiritual and physical oblivion.

The author divides her task into five engaging chapters. The first, "Psychohistorical Underpinnings of White Supremacy," is an attempt to explain the violent nature of White oppression against African people. With respect to the work of other writers on the subject, Dr. Sutherland views her contribution to the literature as "efforts to fuse psychology and history to explain the dialectic association between the European's psychohistorical traditions and White supremacy." For Dr. Sutherland, the underpinnings of White supremacy have their historical roots in the socioeconomic and psychological make-up of Europeans. In her words:

> Consistent with our major thesis, several of Europe's historical traditions have been adopted to the ongoing needs of the White supremacist. One proposition is that the Europeans' firm adherance to their ancient psychohistorical traditions, including a warlike psychology, the need for property, the pillaging of land, and the Europeans' need to be segregated from others make them obdurately resistant to any significant and profound transformation of their human spirit which engendered White supremacy, particularly at the expense of the African humanity.

These psychohistorical traditions, which aided the rise of global White supremacy, indicate no abatement in terms of White supremacy's violent nature against African peoples.

Employing five orientations (four of which are nonideal—the nonstruggler, the reactive struggler, the opportunistic individual, the partially committed struggler, and one which is an ideal—the authentic struggler), the second chapter, "The Role of the Individual in the Liberating Struggle," presents the end result of the unfolding of the scenario of what Aime Cesaire refers to as the "parody of education" in the hands of the colonizer. In his *Discourse on Colonialism*, Aime Cesaire intimates that the "parody of education (is) the hasty manufacture of a few thousand subordinate functionaries, 'boys,' artisans, office clerks, and interpreters necessary for the smooth operation of business." Or, as he reiterated in that same work, "I am talking about millions of men in whom fear has been cunningly instilled, who have been taught to have an inferiority complex, to tremble, kneel, despair, and behave like flunkeys..." Liberation in the hands of the nonideal types would not allow for what Amilcar Cabral described as a "return to the source," or Hord's "reconstructing memory," and/or what Wa Thiong'o sees as a "rediscovery of the real language of humankind. The language of struggle..."

In the words of Fanon, the ideal type, the committed struggler, edges the African World in the direction of being able to "reconsider the question of cerebral reality and of the cerebral mass of humanity, whose connections must be increased, whose channels must be diversified, and whose message must be rehumanized."

In Chapter Three, "The Marginalization of the African World," the author addresses the historical and contemporary violent nature of White supremacy as it wrecks havoc around the world on the life chances of people of African descent. In the author's view, "...the oppressive global experiences of Africans have resulted in cumulative effects that have frustrated the collective goals of African liberation...(and consequently) people of

African descent have developed various dysfunctional attitudes and behaviors in response to their marginalized status in a world controlled by White supremacy"

Chapter Four, "Anti-African Practices and Diasporan Africans," does essentially what its title states: it draws on evidence of White tyranny directed against people of African descent in countries of which they are residents. In an opening statement Dr. Sutherland wrote: "It is a truism that black skin color has been a stimulus for White tyranny in the West"

The final chapter, "Reclaiming African Cultural Traditions for the Liberation of People of African Descent," is in the vein of Cabral's *Return to the Source*, and mirrors the ideas behind the Black Consciousness Movement of Steven Biko in South Africa as it sought to "rebuild and recondition the mind of the oppressed..." It reflects the ideas of Ngugi Wa Thiong'o in that it is a "rediscovery of the real language of humankind. The language of struggle..." With her pen as the sword and with the African spirit as the driving force, Dr. Sutherland calls us to arms. If we are to defuse the "cultural bomb," reconstruct memory, and checkmate White supremacy, then we must heed the words of our dear sister and move most expeditiously to join the struggle.

Wa Thiong'o writes "Struggle makes history. Struggle makes us. In struggle is our history, our language and our being. That struggle begins wherever we are; in whatever we do; then we become part of those millions whom Martin Carter once saw sleeping not to dream but dreaming to change the world."

In his book *Black Skin, White Masks*, which for the author was an attempt at a psychoanalytical interpretation of the Black problem, Frantz Fanon concluded his introductory chapter with the following statement:

> ...my observations and my conclusions (in the book) are valid only for the Antilles...at least concerning the black man at home. Another book could be dedicated to explaining the differences that separate the Negro of the Antilles from the Negro in Africa (and elsewhere in the African diaspora).

It is my feeling that Dr. Marcia Sutherland's work is that book.

A. J. Williams-Myers
Acting Chair/Black Studies
The College at New Paltz
State University of New York

Acknowledgments

This book was completed due to the love, encouragement, and support of my family, friends, and colleagues. I am especially grateful to my late friend and colleague Jerome Thornton for his faith in my ideas and for his unflinching support of this book. I am also deeply indebted and grateful to Daudi Azibo, Jules Harrell, Asa Hilliard, Kwasi Sarfoh, and A. J. Williams-Myers, all of whom reviewed chapters and offered me constructive and generous feedback. I am, to be sure, responsible for any errors of content or judgment.

Special thanks to Deborah Curry from whom I received invaluable library assistance. I wish to thank Barbara McCaskill for sharing her ideas with me on how to improve this work. I am especially thankful to Sisa Moyo for her thorough editing and generous comments on this work. Also, my thanks to Tracy Gaithers, Gary Cross, and Reginald Hicks for their research assistance.

To my colleagues in the Association of Black Psychologists, special gratitude for validating my ideas and for your sustained encouragement. To Mari Evans, my heartfelt love and thanks for all your support.

Finally, my bedrock of unconditional love and support has been my family. My deepest gratitude and love. To all those unnamed, I am thankful for your contribution to this work.

Chapter 1

Psychohistorical Underpinnings of White Supremacy

The great prophecy of the Mossi turned out to be the prophecy of all of Africa: "When the first white man appears in the land—the nation will die."

Chancellor Williams
The Destruction of Black Civilization

The appearance of the settler has meant in terms of syncretism the death of the aboriginal society, cultural lethargy, and petrification.

Frantz Fanon
The Wretched of the Earth

Africans had prospered for many millennia until the coming of alien and hostile Arab, Asian, and European invaders. In 1675 B.C. the Hyksos or shepherd kings invaded Africa from Western Asia, which is now referred to as the Middle East. The Hyksos were followed by the European invaders who came in 332 B.C. (Clarke, 1991) and by the Arab assault on Africa which began in the seventh century. From medieval times, Arabs have demonstrated anti-African attitudes and practices which have resulted in the hostile expropriation of African territory and the enslavement and continuous oppression of Africans. The Arab enslavement trade, which sought to conquer, deafricanize, and arabize Africa, began a thousand years before the European enslavement trade. According to Clarke (1991), "the Arab slave trade, using Islam as its rallying cry, drained Africa of its vitality and energy so that it lacked the ability to withstand the European enslavers" (p. 380). One should never underestimate the long-standing Arab hostility displayed towards Africans.

The evidence is however obscure on the specific period in history when Black skin color first served as a stimulus for these invaders' tyranny (Lewis, 1990). Consensus opinion is that by the early fifteenth century Europeans were the primary group to unleash their explosive racist assaults on the humanity of people of African descent. In that era, after more than a thousand years of grandeur, once powerful and autonomous West Africans were also threatened by internal strife and were unable to successfully defend against the hostile Europeans who invaded their territories.

Many writers have discussed the varied ways that over three thousand years of European cultural, economic, physical, psychological, social, and spiritual assaults have impacted the global existence of people of African descent. There is also a well-documented literature of the Europeans' relentless struggle to take from us whatever we have of human worth including our history, our bodies, our material wealth, and our identity (Bennett, 1981; Davidson, 1961; Jackson, 1970; James, 1985; Rodney, 1972).

It is beyond the scope of this chapter to go into a detailed analysis of the pseudoscientific theories and other self deluding and immoral assumptions used by the oppressors to justify and rationalize their brutalization, exploitation, and domination of Africans (see Yeboah, 1988; Bernal, 1987). However, Kennedy (1987) is a good example. He viewed the rise of White supremacy as the result of a complex set of motives, personal gain, national glory, religious zeal, and a sense of adventure. For him, "many societies in their time have thrown up individuals and groups willing to dare all and do anything in order to make the world their oyster. What distinguished the captains, crews, and explorers of Europe was that they possessed the ships and the firepower with which to achieve their ambitions, and that they came from a political environment in which competition, risk, and entrepreneurship were prevalent" (p. 28).

Kennedy's analysis is flawed for a number of reasons. First, he has ignored the convincing evidence that Africans were among the most adventurous of peoples and probably traveled to Europe around 40,000 B.C. (Clegg, 1987). Kennedy also failed to address the firm evidence that the earliest cultures of Europe were shaped by the artistic, cultural, political, religious, and technological contributions of ancient Black Egypt (James, 1985; Van Sertima, 1986). Finally, Kennedy's reliance on favorable motives to define White supremacy is questionable. Du Bois (1976) writes that the evidence is strong that "mechanical power, not deep human emotion or creative genius nor ethical concepts of justice, has made Europe ruler of the world" (p. 149).

This book will demonstrate that White supremacy was developed and maintained through Europeans displaying their nefarious psychohistorical traditions in the context of the African world. The primary objective of this discussion is to trace the psychohistorical factors which allow for the unconscientious treatment of Africans by Europeans. There is a significant body of writings on the foundations of Europeans' anti-African attitudes, ideologies, policies, and practices (Diop, 1974; Fredrickson, 1981; Welsing, 1970; Wright, 1975). This writer's contribution to the literature lies in the effort to fuse psychology and history to explain the dialectic association between the Europeans' psychohistorical traditions and White supremacy.

In this discussion White supremacy is defined as the varied manifestations of violence imposed on people of African descent by Europeans for the satisfaction of the Europeans' maleficient psychohistorical needs. By the "varied manifestations of violence" we are concerned with the Europeans' utilization of cultural, economic, ideological, military, political, psychological, religious, and social means to dominate Africans and uphold White privilege, power, and wealth. Moreover, we hope to demonstrate how White supremacy has its origin and development primarily in the subjective and material consequences for Europeans from acting out their ancestral customs in the context of the African world.

In exploring several psychohistorical underpinnings of global White supremacy, the primordial mentality, desire to be segregated, deep-rooted need for property, and warlike psychology of Europeans will be examined. Europeans' response to White supremacy will also be presented, along with a discussion on how people of African descent ought to respond to the weight of the psychohistorical findings related to White supremacy.

To leave no doubts about my intentions, this writer strongly insists that for the oppressed of African descent to clearly see our way to liberation we must take seriously the blatant, blaring psychohistorical evidence on the nature of our European oppressors. We must cease in our underestimation of the psychohistorical immoral resources of those Europeans who have not relinquished their long-standing role as the enemies of people of African descent.

Natural Conditions and the Psychology of Europeans

The psychology of a people forms out of a variety of general factors including biological, historical, and societal circumstances. In exploring the psychohistorical underpinnings of White supremacy, the preponderance of the evidence lends support to the assertion that Europeans' earliest existence in the cold and hostile physical environment of the northern Eurasian steppes allowed violent-aggressive, segregating, predatory, materialistic, and Napoleonic tendencies to become deeply rooted in the psyche of group members. Furthermore, as they migrated across Europe, the ancient Europeans encountered other ferocious natural conditions (Barker, 1906; Bradley, 1978; Diop, 1974; Van Sertima, 1986). We contend that protracted harsh natural environments played a prominent role in determining the persistence of the abovementioned maleficent psychohistorical values across generations of Europeans. For centuries Europeans also led a profoundly selfish, nomadic existence which contributed to the development of these European cultural traditions. The psychological features which developed out of these two primary sources of experiences, that is adapting to inimical material conditions and leading an individualistic and selfish nomadic existence, were to aid in the determination and maintenance of European power, privilege, and wealth.

Early Europeans were unique among the human races in their engagement in thousand of years of struggle for survival against the cruelties of the glacial epochs (Bradley, 1978; Breasted, 1935). The Ice Age existence of prehistoric Caucasians, the ferocity of nature on the Eurasian steppes, and the scarcity of vital resources meant a relentless and uncertain life or death struggle. To be sure, as Diop (1974) stated, "in the unrewarding activity that the physical environment imposed on man, there was already implied materialism...and the secular spirit" (p. 112). Believing either that matter was the basic reality of the universe or that everything can be shown to derive ultimately from matter, the European's materialistic outlook was to have devastating consequences on the African world. Their protracted and aggressive psychological adaptations to the struggle with purely material and physical forces retarded their rising to higher human involvement in the realm of moral values. Consequently the will to aggression and the will to materialistic aggrandizement became sovereign in the European tradition.

The early beginnings of Caucasians led Diop (1987) to remark that "crime, violence, war and a taste for risk, so many sentiments born of the climate and the early conditions of existence, all predisposed the Aryan world, extraordinary as this may appear to a great historical destiny" (p. 163).

Moreover, Diop (1974) has elucidated the fundamental human responses to environmental conditions which were to influence the historical relations between Europeans and Africans. He wrote that "the European learned to rely on himself alone and his own possibilities...they were instinctively to love conquest, because of a desire to escape from those hostile surroundings. The milieu chased them away; they had to leave it or succumb, try to conquer a place in a more clement nature. Invasions would not cease, once an initial contact with the Black world of the South had taught them the existence of a land where the living was easy, riches abundant, technique flourishing" (p. 112).

It is possible to discuss the influences of physical environmental conditions on both individual and group behavior. For example, while cognizant of the multifarious variables that affect personality, Rose (1912) suggested that the conquering and strenuous nature of Napoleon Bonaparte, the eighteenth century French ruler, could be attributed to his homeland Corsica. Rose reasoned that "The unrest of the sea, the awesomeness of the mountains, are balanced by no glad and careless life in fertile plains" (p. 3). He added that "Napoleon would not have gone so far had he not early been inured to war and hardship. Corsica made him a warrior" (p. 8).

It is instructive to point out that in his expansionistic thrusts to rule the world, Napoleon was distinguished by his firm reliance on "mere dry calculation, and his despise for moral and physical obstacles" (Rose, 1912). His personality was imbued with power drives such that he is reported to have stated: "Power is my mistress! The conquest of that mistress has cost me so much that I will allow no one to rob me of her, or to share her with me!" (Nehru, 1982, p. 381).

At another level, Hertz (1970) stated that the whole course of history shows that the Teutons, Celts, Persians, and other European and Arab groups were driven to marauding and conquest by the inclemency of their desert and mountain homelands. He indicated that worldly power became prominent over spiritual power for these warlike groups. It must be noted that several of our historical European oppressors, including the Portuguese and the White South Afrikaners, are purported to have their ancestral roots in these conquering races. The Portuguese are reported to come from the Celts-Iberian family, while the earliest Dutch are of Celtic-Gaul descent (Motley, 1898). The ancestry of South Afrikaners can be traced back to Dutch, German, French, and other northern European groups whose traditions were to figure prominently in the attitudes and behaviors of these early colonizers.

Barker (1906) wrote that the Dutch Netherlands were inhabited by people who "lived by the sea, and who by a constant fight with nature, had become determined, warlike and even ferocious" (p. 90). The earliest Dutch engaged in fishing and trade primarily because of the natural poverty of their country's soil and the inclemency of weather. By the 1600s they had achieved maritime and trade supremacy and were also exercising colonial power over many people, including Africans. By 1609 the Dutch were said to have employed 120 ships in the African enslavement trade along the West African coastline. Their global supremacy was facilitated by the aboriginal warlike, self-reliant, determined, and individualistic spirit of the Dutch. For some writers it was the Dutch peoples' mammonism of the most selfish kind which directed the decline of the Netherlands in the 1800s (Barker, 1906).

The South Afrikaner Boers, descendants of the ancient Dutch, have sought for the perpetuation of White supremacy by steadfastly refusing to cleanse their psyche of the abovecited psychohistorical customs. Instead, they remain determined to protect the material interests of the White privileged population.

Perhaps it is of some utility to indicate that individuals whose tendency it is to prevaricate on the topic of White supremacy will object to our general approach on several predictable grounds. We anticipate that there are those who will object to what they view as our exaggerated environmental determinism. Others will accuse us of genetic determinism. We might also be charged with presenting a racist paradigm. These claims are fictitious.

We certainly recognize that cultural, economic, military, social, and political forces cooperated with the Europeans' ancestral propensities to produce and maintain global White supremacy. There is no inflexible predestination for Caucasians to engage in White tyranny against people of African descent. As people become increasingly conscious of themselves, creative imagination, free will, and intent allow them to choose the bases on which they will conduct their human relations. It is the individual who decides how flexible s(he) will be in responding both to their historical past and to the characteristics of their cultural context.

However, there can be no refuting the fact that global White supremacy is axiomatic. The White supremacist has always intended to rule over or annihilate people of African descent. Undoubtedly, as Williams (1976) affirms, the White supremacist is the "implacable foe, the traditional and everlasting enemy" (p. 329) of African peoples. Consistent with our major thesis, several of Europe's historical traditions have been adopted to the ongoing needs of the White supremacist.

A Warlike Psychology

There is no lack of historical examples of the violent and warlike psychology of Europeans which motivates them to seek the satisfaction of their narcissistically defined self-interests (Caesar, 1917; Kennedy, 1987; Livy, 1919; Tacitus, 1931). Europeans have historically viewed themselves as the conquering and unconquerable race. The preponderance of the evidence also confirms that Europeans do not easily believe in the unselfish sharing of the world's resources and power (Robinson, Gallagher, and Denny, 1961; Bennett, 1981; Kennedy, 1987). It is a quite plausible postulate that these fundamental beliefs coupled with primordial aggressive impulses have been the fundamental determinants of the White supremacists' expansionistic and imperialistic behaviors.

For instance, in his examination of the world since 1500, Kennedy's (1987) research revealed that the "egoistic nature of the European states meant that prolonged peace was unusual and that within a few years preparations were being made for further campaigning" (p. 85). The aim of such campaigning was to expand territorial boundaries and to galvanize national economies. Herodotus (1928) wrote, "I have remarked that the Thracians, the Scyths, the Persians, the Lydians, and almost all other barbarians, hold the citizens who practice trades and their children in less repute than the rest, while they esteem as noble those who keep aloof from handicrafts and especially honor such as are given wholly to war. These ideas prevail throughout the whole of Greece" (p. 140). According to Diop (1991), in ancient Sparta the state had ownership of newborns and would order that they be fed to predators if they had any physical malformation making them unfit for military service in defense of the state. The Roman Consul Cininnatus aptly summarized the psychology of the ancient Europeans, and to a considerable extent the psychology of their contemporary offsprings, when he commented that "we are somehow fated to enjoy the favor of gods in larger measure when warring than when at peace" (Livy, 1919, p. 69).

Elaborating on early Roman society, Livy asserted that "it was not a man's right that determined his conduct, but the confidence he had in his strength; and one had to make good by force what one meant to do" (p. 39). Lady Lugard (1964) informed us that after the breakup of the Roman empire, countless hoards of northern European nomads, "unacquainted with the gentler arts of civilization, but vigorous and active in their barbarism, awaited nothing but the opportunity of conquest" (p. 34).

Similarly, Julius Caesar (1917) indicated during the Gallic War that, "... from every corner of Gaul a great host of desperadoes and brigands had gathered, whom the hope of plunder and passion for war seduced from the daily toil of agriculture" (p. 161). As Caesar (1917) pointed out, the German state enforced the yearly migration of its citizens such that they "might not be tempted by continuous association to substitute agriculture for their warrior zeal" (p. 347). "It was easier," said Motley (1898), "to summon the Germans to the battlefield than to ploy" (p. 7). Caesar's ideas on the constancy of the race characteristics of Gauls and Germans have been challenged (Hertz, 1970). Yet, the recent unification of Germany raised anxieties in many quarters. Indeed, news media commentators have been debating if the Germans can be trusted to preserve world peace (Bellak, 1990; Friedman, 1990; Rosenthal, 1990; Schmemann, 1990).

Clearly, Europeans believe that the world belongs to the strong and not to the weak, and that who is stronger can only be known by fighting. There is also evidence which suggests that in the struggle for existence, Europeans have viewed war as a biological necessity. One thesis is that "war is the supreme agent of the evolutionary process...the one test mankind has yet contrived of a nation's fitness to survive" (Tucker, 1968, p. 156). In the European perspective of practical affairs, might and right are synonymous.

The warlike ferocity of Europeans is said to be reflected in several of their contemporary cultural symbols. Nehru (1942) indicated that the national character of several European groups is embodied in the aggressive fighting animals (beasts of prey) which serve as national symbols. These include the eagle of Germany and the United States, the lion and bulldog of Britain, the fighting cock of France, and the Russian bear. For Nehru, people living with these as symbols are in essence people who "strike up aggressive attitudes, roar and prey on others" (p. 15).

One major thesis is that from prehistoric to contemporary times it is possible to discern veritable continuities in the thought-behavioral patterns of Europeans from which global White supremacy has derived benefits. The research findings overwhelmingly confirm our suspicions that Europeans hostile relations with people of African descent is a modern twist on a very old tale.

Europeans' firm adherence to their ancient psychohistorical traditions, including a warlike psychology, the need for property, the pillaging of land, and the Europeans' need to be segregated from others, makes them obdurately resistant to a significant and profound transformation of their human spirit which engendered White supremacy. For centuries Europeans have ensured the transmission of their anti-African violence to each of their generations. For example, the transatlantic enslavement trade in Africans was viewed by Europeans as a great education for the European youth. Enslavers were reported to have reasoned: "... think of the effect, the result of a slave voyage on a youngster starting in his teens...what an education was such a voyage for the lad. What an enlargement of experience for a country boy. If he returned to the farm his whole outlook in life would be changed. He went out a boy; he returned a man" (as quoted by Williams, 1980, p. 47). It is also the case that while Europeans have brought wars and miseries to the African world, White youths have traditionally been taught that Africans were the enemies of Christianity, democracy, and civilization. By extension, Whites have historically socialized their youth to see themselves as the upholders of civilization (Caute, 1983; Moore-King, 1988). These practices obviously persist to protect the Europeans' monopoly of power and wealth, to satisfy their need to control the world and its resources, and to uphold the self-generated myth of their grandeur.

In his treatise on the Zimbabwean independence war of the 1970s, Bruce Moore-King (1988) asserted that the White elders told their sons they were fighting a "war that was a glorious adventure, an easy test of manhood, a war that was right and always honorable, a war where the good were White and the evil were black, a war as simple as that" (p. 3). Moore-King concluded that the White elders "valued the comfort of their life styles beyond the lives of their own children, beyond the lives of any children. They did not want to share. It was for greed they sent us, the battered generation, to war" (p. 113).

Religion and White Supremacy

Many Caucasians profess a relationship with a Supreme and righteous Creator. It has been said that 90 percent of White Afrikaans speakers are members of the Dutch Reformed church, an institution which has been instrumental in propagating racist ideologies. Likewise, in spite of Whites' participation in maintaining the racial status quo in the United States, a *Newsweek* article reported that 76 percent of Americans polled thought they had a good chance of getting to heaven (Woodward, 1989). Whites, argued James Cone (1987), can only think in White thought-patterns, even in reference to God.

One certainly must not overlook the Europeans' longstanding reliance on Christianity to obtain gratification of their maleficent psychohistorical needs. Consistent with our discussion on the materialistic tendency of Europeans, the early Roman Christians viewed the universe as corrupt. For them, "the creation is the work of an evil godling, the demiurge, who trapped a spark of goodness in matter; and that there is a perpetual war for the redemption of the divine spark in every man from the darkness of the evil visible universe" (Smith, 1971, p. 42). Roman beliefs contrasted with those of ancient Africans, such as the Egyptians, who saw the whole universe as being infused with intelligence and goodness. The Egyptian Plotinus was reported to have accused the Romans of being morally bankrupt and therefore lacking in any real knowledge of God. The ancient Egyptians held that without real moral strength, God is only a word (Smith, 1971). The course of history was to support these observations on the White supremacists' theology.

In his expansionistic thrusts, the Roman ruler Constantine was said to believe that "God had committed to him the government of all terrestrial affairs" (Smith, 1971, p. 158-167). Constantine's aim was a universal church—a Catholic world empire—and ancient African culture suffered gravely during his reign. As they moved from place to place, Constantine's imperial troops, with the cross of Christ as their emblem, slaughtered Africans. Constantine also displayed his commitment to the destruction of traditional African religious beliefs and practices.

It is of interest to point out that during the rise of Christianity in Rome, baptism was the accepted indicator of true faith in Christ. Constantine was said to have been baptized on his death bed, opening question as to whether or not he had any true faith in Christ (Smith, 1971). For our purposes, Constantine affirmatively responded to his conquering, predatory, warlike, and materialistic ancestral customs.

The early Roman church was also responsible for labeling as pagans and infidels all those who did not convert to Catholic Christianity. The Roman ruler Gratian (A.D. 375-383) began the brutal persecution of all pagans. Theodosius I (A.D. 379-395), who viewed himself as God's agent, issued antipagan laws which provided justification for the immoral behavior of Europeans who were intent on using Christianity to satisfy their psychohistorical needs. Under Theodosius' rule, Christianity and Roman citizenship were coterminous (Barker, 1966). Like his predecessors, Theodosius and his followers displayed wanton greed after material gain and were not spiritually motivated. The African world fell victim to yet another glaring example of the evil genius of Europeans (Clarke, 1991). When Theodosius' followers knew that an area had something that could be plundered, these predators would arbitrarily declare that sacrifices and dreadful rites took place there; greed after gain led the monks to plunder the Serapeum of Egypt to the extent that they even took away the floors (King, 1960). The orthodoxy established by Theodosius was used by other Roman rulers to further pillage and destroy the African world for their own material well-being.

Justinian I, who officially took the Roman throne in A.D. 527, was to surpass all other Roman rulers in his quest to use Christianity in order to rule the world. Justinian dealt severely with the African world. Under his rule the Egyptians, Nubians, Ethiopians and other ancient Africans were ruthlessly persecuted, the Egyptian sanctuaries of Isis and Osiris were destroyed, ancient priests were arrested and their sacred images were sent to Constantinople, and our ancestors' cultural centers and classical educational systems and institutions were closed (Barker, 1966). Clarke (1991) indicated that in the early persecution of Christians more Africans were killed in the amphitheaters of North Africa than in the arenas of Rome.

Black skin was to become the exclusive mark of the pagan, racially inferior, uncivilized being. Christianity provided a moral justification for the enslavement, colonization, and perpetual domination of Africans. "Europeans justified enslaving Blacks on the grounds that it gave the infidels the opportunity to cast off their heathenism and embrace Christian religion, a rationalization that extended well into the modern era" (Woods, 1990, p. 35). In sum, hatred of Blacks is found among those Caucasians who do and do not have a relationship with God. Caucasians seem to not only believe that God's love "invariably shores up outrageous sociopolitical structures that want Blacks to be complacent and obedient to White enemies" (Cone, 1987, p. 72), but also that God sanctions the righteousness of their destruction of Blacks. Writers such as Carter G. Woodson (1939) maintain that racial autocracy is the supreme divinity of Europeans.

White Supremacy and the African World

Examining the historical relationship between Europeans and the African world, there is no doubt that White supremacy owes its legitimacy to the persistent recapitulations of the European's violent, expansionistic, and materialistic traditions. Some of the oppressed of African descent have been acutely aware of the "violence with which the supremacy of White values is affirmed and the aggressiveness which has permeated the victory of these values over the ways of life and thoughts of the native" (Fanon, 1963, p. 43).

The evidence is quite clear that Europeans' unmitigated violence and greed after gain facilitated the physical captures of Africans which began in the fifteenth century. The historical records show that Europe's plantation economies in the New World needed labor and resorted to African labor because it was the cheapest and best.

Africans' relative immunity to diseases also contributed to their enslavement (Rawley, 1981; Williams, 1980). In addition, slavery in the modern era was diminishing throughout the world, and consequently attention became focused on Africa (Manning, 1990). For Williams (1976), the great revolt of White slaves, the Manelukes in A.D. 1250 and these slaves' murderous assaults against their Turk and Arab masters ended forever the general enslavement of Whites, and thereafter led to a concentration on the enslavement of Blacks only.

This writer concurs with those who suggest that Black skin color did not necessarily create the oppression of people of African descent (Chinweizu, 1975). Among other factors, military weaknesses, alliance with the oppressors, disunity and disorganized responses to White invaders have historically weakened the African world's ability to counter the varied manifestations of the Europeans' psychohistorical traditions.

Pertaining to military affairs, as was discussed earlier, the Europeans' historical legacy reveals their belief that "providence is on the side of great battalions" (Rose, 1912, p. 249). For the

European, there is "nothing unjust or immoral in subduing others and appropriating their possessions. They believe that they were only following the universal law of nature, which commands the weak to obey the strong" (Barker, 1906, p. 290). As it pertains to the African world, the oppressors utilization of military armaments have historically aided White tyranny against Africans during the transatlantic enslavement period, and the subsequent colonial and postcolonial periods. Beginning around A.D. 1400, only Europeans and Arabs were able to obtain the limited supply of guns (Kodjo, 1987). From these earliest times to this day, continental Africa has received secondary and inferior military supplies from the West, while Africans in the diaspora suffer from military unpreparedness. These circumstances limit Africans' means of action.

People of African descent have demonstrated that the oppressors can be fought and defeated despite their superiority of weapons. The historical examples include the victories of the Maroons of Jamaica over the British enslavers in the mid 1700s, the Haitian revolution (1791-1804) which resulted in the defeat of the French enslavers, the Ethiopians defeat of Mussolini's forces at Adowa in 1896, and the numerous military victories of the Ashantis of Ghana over the British colonists during the nineteenth century. More recently, there is the Kenyan Mau Mau fighters' military successes during the 1950s against the White British settlers and in the 1970s the Guineas' guerrilla victory against the Portuguese settlers, the Mozambicans' victory over the Portuguese colonists, and the Zimbabweans' victory over the British White settlers. All provide examples of how Africans can use inferior weapons to defeat Europeans.

Some argue that the Africans' armed struggles for independence from colonial rule were given impetus because European states such as France, Belgium, Portugal, and Spain, weakened by the European wars of 1914 and 1939, had lost the will to support White settlers in the colonial outposts of Africa (Mazrui and Tidy, 1984). Notwithstanding these arguments, people of African descent have historically shown their abilities to wage successful struggles against European hegemony. Despite such victories, as will be demonstrated in other chapters, White hegemony at the expense of African humanity remains entrenched in the world order. Our racial oppression is constant because we remain powerless.

One can appreciate when Edem Kodjo (1987) states that "it is because there are no defense policies in Africa, and because African armies—with very few exceptions—are not meaningful in the modern sense of the word—Africa remains the privileged field of expansion for the world powers" (p. 252). Most African states have failed to form alliances with each other against the Europeans. This failure has not only served to weaken African states militarily, but it has also allowed the oppressors to "play one African power against the other and to defeat each one in isolation" (Adu Boahen, 1987). Hence the valid argument that Africa must have a unified defense system—an African High Command (Clarke, 1991). No nation, as Clarke wrote, "is really independent and free until its people can defend themselves and become the instruments of their liberation. Nationhood and freedom are not gifts that are handed down from one generation to another. Each generation, in its own way, must secure its nationhood and freedom with its own hands" (p. 287). For some thinkers, to ensure independence and security, Africans owe it to themselves to "accede to the equalizing power of the atom" (Chinweizu, 1975; Kodjo, 1987).

Africans as Europeans' Property

Europeans' primordial protests against their earliest harsh beginnings made property rights over human rights central in European culture. This was to play a crucial part in the racial subordination of Africans and the development of White supremacy.

Dating from antiquity, as we have seen, white-skinned Indo-Aryans from the northern hostile cradle behaved as if their own safety and survival as a people depended on their migrating to and aggressively invading the richer and more advanced southern (Black) cradle (Diop, 1974; Williams, 1976). It is also the case that the Europeans' Faustian soul, that is their desire to extend their power and to master the world and its resources, made it possible for them to define the purpose of life as the expansion of the self through the acquisition of property, including human property.

Based on the psychohistorical thesis of the Europeans construing the world in material terms, it was certainly consistent for them to have dehumanized Africans to the level of material things. The enslavement of Africans was based on and justified by the fundamental principle that people of African descent were the property of Whites.

Historically Europeans have repudiated the sacredness of the African's human existence. To illustrate, we note that on the British slave ship *Zong*, Captain Luke Collingwood, on his way to Jamaica from St. Thomas on the African coast, lied that he was short of water and threw 132 Africans overboard. During the voyage many Africans were dying of natural causes. The British law stated that if Africans died a natural death, the ship owners would be responsible for the loss. In contrast, if the enslaved were thrown overboard on the pretext that the ships' safety depended on this, the underwriters would assume the cost (Fryer, 1984). Following Collingwood's inhumane actions, the ship owners brought an action for insurance on the grounds that the loss of African slaves was congruent with the clause of the policy which insured against "perils of the sea." The British court concluded that the case of slaves was the same as if horses had be thrown overboard. Damages of thirty pounds were awarded for each slave (Hoare, 1828). Williams (1980) postulated that "the idea that the captain and crew could be persecuted for mass homicide never entered into this scenario" (p. 46). Shameful repetitions of this traditional racist mentality persist under global White supremacy.

In 1977 Basil Rowlands, a White Rhodesian farmer, was accused of kicking a sixty-five-year old African man to death.

Rowlands subsequently pleaded that he was displeased with the manner in which the man was planting maize pips along a furrow. V. J. Kock, the Magistrate at Salisbury Regional Court, argued that although the consequences had been unfortunate, he did not consider the assault a serious one. Rowlands was sentenced to a fine of $(R) three hundred or two months in jail (Caute, 1983, p. 132).

In the United States the race of murder victims—and therefore their status and worth—is the primary predictor of death verdicts. Those who murder Whites are more likely to be sentenced to death than those who murder Blacks. In 1990 Blacks were homicide victims at a rate almost six times that of Whites, yet, of the twenty-three condemned men put to death, only 5 percent were executed for killing Black people. Other statistics show that since the United States resumed capital punishment in 1977, of the 144 people executed, approximately 87 percent of them had White victims (Kroll, 1991). Greenberg (1993) recently reminded us that America's former slaveholding and segregating states are primarily responsible for the executions of Black Americans who kill Whites. He also wrote that, "since 1932, when records were first kept, only one White man who killed a Black has been executed."

The evidence on Europeans' repudiation of the sacredness of the lives of people of African descent is one consequence of the violence of White supremacy. As we have noted, Europeans have fleshed out their expansionistic, predatory, and materialistic propensities in the context of the African world by their enslavement, colonization, and perpetual domination of people of African descent. To justify their brutality, Europeans have weaved a web of ideas to perpetuate and maintain both the myths of European superiority and African inferiority.

Pillaging of Land

Another nefarious consequence of White supremacy is the expropriation of Africa's geographic space by Europeans.

Europeans are numerically less than the other races of the earth, however their psychohistorical traditions, particularly militaristic action, have enabled European nations to control three-fifths of the world's land. Eurocentric control of the destinies of the other two-fifths is maintained through various blatant and hidden political mechanisms (Kodjo, 1987).

Since antiquity, Africa has been the objective of land hungry European barbarians. For instance, in A.D. 429 the Vandals entered North Africa and ten years later established a German state at Carthage (Barker, 1966). By the 1800s, various European nations had annexed portions of Africa's soil. At the Berlin Conference of 1884-1885 European core instincts resulted in the partitioning of continental Africa. The Berlin Conference did not initiate the scramble for Africa but merely accelerated the race for colonies that had begun in the fifteenth and sixteenth centuries (Adu Boahen, 1987; Clarke, 1991). By 1939, with Ethiopia being occupied by the Italians, and Liberia standing as a semi-colonial state which fell prey to American economic imperialism, no section of Africa was truly independent (Mazrui and Tidy, 1989).

The cultural, economical, moral, political, psychological, and social devastations experienced by Africans as a result of the Berlin Conference are beyond the purviews of this chapter. These issues are more fully addressed in this book's chapter on the marginalization of the African world. More pressing to the immediate focus is the notion that it would be foolish, for the oppressed of African descent to entertain the thought that a historical accident occurred in the winter of 1884-1885.

Well-documented history shows the immoral ends to which several European groups went to expropriate the Africans' land. European countries including Germany, Portugal, Italy, Britain, Spain, France, and the United States garnered massive accumulations of capital from their plunders of the agricultural and mineral wealth of Africa. Moreover, the exploitation of Africans' physical and psychological resources was of vast underlying importance in Europe's transition from mercantile to industrial capitalism (Rodney, 1972). In brief, duplicity, military pacification techniques, treachery, forced signatures, and treaties by irresponsible African persons and a unilateral interpretation of such agreements by Europeans were the normative approaches of Europeans to acquire Africa (Howe, 1966; Woodson, 1939).

South Africa provides a useful representation of the psychology informing the Europeans' practice of expropriating the African continent. During the early colonial period, the policies of the Dutch East Indian Company ensured that only Whites owned land. When the indigenous African population challenged the attempts to disown them of their lands, the Europeans responded with brute force (De Villiers, 1987). In 1791 van Jaarsveld, one of the Boers' leaders, is reported to have relied on treachery to acquire the land of the indigenous Xhosa by scattering tobacco on the ground in front of a group of Xhosa and having them all shot when they stooped down to pick it up (De Villiers, 1987).

Other preconditions of Afrikaner nationalism included Whites' misconception that Boers and their descendants were by natural right entitled to as much of the indigenous Africans' land as they wanted and needed. Some Europeans, having the need to justify their predatory behaviors, convinced themselves that the land was ownerless. Afrikaners have also considered the heartland theirs by right of conquest. Believing that physical labor should not be done by Whites, they have forced the indigenous people to labor as slaves. Other immoral assumptions which informed Whites' possession of Black South Africa include the Afrikaners' belief that "political superiority was theirs by natural right and the immoral assumption that uncivilized Black culture would give way before superior White will" (De Villiers, 1987, p. 62).

Some thinkers have sought to rationalize the avarice and violence of Europeans by the promotion of these traditions to the status of human needs. Niebuhr (1934) argued that "every group as every individual has expansive desires which are rooted in the instinct of survival and soon extend beyond it. The 'will to live' becomes the 'will to power'" (p. 18). He also concluded that greed, the will to power, and other forms of self-assertion are natural impulses that can never be controlled or sublimated by reason. For us, Niebhur's statements are representative of Eurocentric, paternalistic scholarship.

Africans have voiced the fact that they have a totally different value system from Europeans. For instance, the ancient Ethiopian Sabacos, who invaded and ruled Egypt for fifty years, voluntarily retired from Egypt after he had been terrified by a dream that he had committed sacrilege by putting Egyptian priests to death. The Aborigines, who sometimes refer to themselves as "blackfellas," were reportedly a nonmaterialistic and noncompetitive people (Mydans, 1988). In precolonial times, similar to other African groups, the Aborigines had no sense of private property. They believed in collective ownership and equal accessibility to the land and its resources. These indigenous beliefs brought the Aborigines into conflict with the land-hungry British convicts who settled in Australia and used vile and inhumane measures to expropriate the land (Tucker, 1968).

The Segregating Tendency

It is important to emphasize the cultural differences which exist between Europeans and Africans. A prevalent feature of anti-Black attitudes and behaviors is the White supremacists' strong psychological need to separate themselves from people of African descent. This is another recapitulation of an ancient European cultural tradition from which White supremacy has derived benefits.

Prehistoric writings show that in early Europe humans lived in smaller groups isolated from each other by wide spaces. According to Diop (1987), among the Aryans, "the nomadic style of life makes of each clan, that is of each family, an absolute entity, an autonomous cell, independent in all its purposes...This situation, born during the nomadic life, perpetuated itself for a long time after sedentarisation" (p. 144). The ancient German was purported to build his "solitary hut where inclination prompted. Close neighborhood was not to his taste" (Motley, 1898, p. 7). We read that the Gauls thought "it the true sign of valour when the neighbors are driven to retire from their lands and no man dares to settle near, and at the same time they believe they will be safer thereby, having removed all fear of a sudden inroad" (Caesar, 1917, p. 349). According to Davidson (1974), the "Vandals, Goths, Franks and Visigoths were men of clannish loyalty for whom the notions of universal culture, a culture capable of embracing many peoples and glowing with the vision of a new society, long remained beyond their grasp" (p. 11).

Racial segregation (apartheid) is a central feature of societies comprised of people of various racial ancestry including Australia, Britain, Brazil, Canada, South Africa, and the United States. South Africa is one stark example of the social and political reality of apartheid. The historical evidence reviewed thus far suggests that the Afrikaner nationalists are responding to an historical consciousness deeply rooted in their ancient past. As aforementioned, the Dutch had a strong influence on the development of the apartheid environment in South Africa.

In the early history of the Netherlands, "each province was a conglomeration of heterogenous parts, cities, estates, lordships, and each part was a separate unit possessing individual rights, privileges, customs of administrations, traditions and jurisdictions" (Barker, 1906, p. 160). Each unit was said to jealously guard its independence, its customs, and its privileges to the extent that collective action against a foreign enemy was impossible. Barker (1906) suggests that each province functioned to advance its own self-interests at the cost of the common good. Hence no authentic and effective unity was said to exist in the Netherlands for a very long time. One possible reason for this phenomenon was that early Dutch construed that cooperation presupposes subordination (Barker, 1906). Despite these contentions, it is critical to point out that "Whites tend to unite no matter what sectional conflicts might otherwise divide them, against nearly all non-Whites" (Davidson, 1974, p. 286).

Similar to their Dutch ancestors, Davidson (1969) wrote that the Dutch who settled at the Cape of Good Hope stubbornly pursued the ideal of every farmer living beyond the sight of his neighbor's smoke. Among the early South African Boers "individuality reigned supreme. Everyone went his own way. Egos were big, tempers short, and the spirit of negotiation and compromise totally absent. The Transvaal trekkers established five separate republics and rose up against one another ten times in the first twenty years of their settlement. Even their church split into three separate factions of the Dutch Reformed Church" (Sparks, 1990, p. 114). Likewise, Thompson's (1985) research on South Africa revealed that "most of the Afrikaners were more concerned with the processes in their particular territories than with identifying with an ethnic group that transcended political boundaries" (p. 3).

In the South African case, apartheid has been validated by the White supremacists on the specious Calvinist worldview that every aspect of life is God's work and that every people has its God given place, its own role to play, its allotted tasks, and its own way of finding its soul. White supremacists further suggest that they have a need to be free of contamination from alien ideas (Crapanzano, 1985). The Afrikaner is insecure, fears alien cultures and is devoted to rugged individualism, which is simply another word for selfishness.

Speciously and immorally grounded is the White segregationists' Social Darwinistic notion that Africans are a lower race, childlike, raw, primitive, savage, uncivilized, or of the bush. The White segregationists view White supremacy as being responsible for the preservation of civilization. Thus, dismantling of segregation would inevitably lead to perceived negatives such as intermarriage. In addition, Europeans deep-seated desire for fiercely White monolithic environments is founded in their belief that they have the inherent right to preserve their own destiny, culture, and language.

It should be noted that the United States and other predominantly White societies do not strictly resemble South Africa in their treatment of Africans, not because of any moral certitude on the part of these Europeans, but because Whites have been in the majority for a significant period of these countries' history. Thus people of African descent no longer pose any threat of numerically overwhelming these Europeans. In fact historians have demonstrated that several of the prominent racial policies of South Africa were inspired by the racial patterns that already existed in countries such as the United States. De jure segregation laws were on the books in this country from the 1890s to 1960s. These statutes preceded South Africa's Native Land Acts of 1913, which restricted racial contacts between Africans and Whites, and that country's segregation laws of 1910-1948. For George Fredrickson (1981), another explanation for America's departure from the course completed by White South Africa is that the abolition of slavery in the United States carried with it a certain heritage of moral idealism that might be violated in practice, but could not be breached in principle without a castastrophic effect on the national self-image.

It is argued that Europeans seek separation from people of African descent so as not to diminish their aggressive and materialistic natures which have historically ensured them power. Diop (1974), Lugard (1964), and other writers have observed that the Europeans' moral values became milder through contact with people of the southern cradle. Separation from Africans also allows Caucasians to leave unchallenged the racial stereotypes they have created to rationalize their oppression of people of African descent. Another viewpoint is that Whites' racial xenophobia is the consequence of the enslavement and colonization of Africans. These historical events have served to instill a tenacious sense of racial superiority to which many Whites still cling.

Frances Cress Welsing has developed a different conceptual model in addressing the power needs of Whites which inform their insistence on racial separation. Welsing (1991) charged that the mass inability of Whites to exist peacefully in close proximity to non-Whites is based on the psychological discomfort experienced by Whites when their "color inadequacy" becomes prominent in the presence of people of color. "The quality of Whiteness is a genetic inadequacy or a relative genetic deficiency state, based upon the genetic inability to produce skin pigments of melanin (which are responsible for all skin color). The vast majority of the world's people are not so afflicted, which suggests color is normal for human beings and color absence is abnormal" (p. 4). Welsing further charged that "Europeans responded psychologically, with a profound sense of numerical inadequacy and color inferiority, in their confrontations with the majority of the world's people—all of whom possessed varying degrees of color-producing capacity" (p. 4). Whites, according to Welsing, then painfully recognize that Blacks are inherently more than equal to them. More significantly, the White segregationist possesses a deep fear of racial extinction by the numerically advanced people of color.

Welsing postulated that the difficulty Whites have in according non-Whites sociopolitical and economic equality within the White supremacist's structure "stems neither from a moral issue nor from political or economic need, but from the fundamental sense of their own unequal condition in regards to their numerical inadequacy and color deficiency" (p. 9).

Europeans' primordial segregating tendency has played itself out in many aspects of the African world. The White segregationist perceives that "Blacks living in White areas would get, in justice, White freedoms and that would mean the end of White freedom. Justice demanded separation" (De Villiers, 1987, 311). Thus, separation from Blacks represents Whites' strong determination to entrench White privileges and power, and to restrict the power and privileges of Africans.

White Responses to White Supremacy

It has been our contention that for several centuries White supremacists have maintained their role as the historical and implacable enemies of people of African descent. History and the contemporary experiences of Africans patently demonstrate that Europeans have been among the primary builders of a world reality wherein the African's skin color remains a stimulus for the oppressors' tyranny (Clarke, 1991; Woods, 1990). In this section we seek to highlight what we consider to be the salient responses of Whites to their oppression of people of African descent.

One popular opinion is that the Europeans' second major war in the modern era (1939-1945) engendered significant declines in White supremacy beliefs and practices. Sparks (1990) wrote that "until World War II, the White Western world took for granted its right to dominate the rest of humankind. With the war more than one hundred new nations came into existence...replacing the old assumption of White superiority with a new concept of the equality and dignity of man....The Western world stood horrified at the evidence of the Holocaust and saw in Germany's crime a grotesque caricature of itself, the ultimate implications of its own inherent master race ideas" (p. 184-186). It is interesting to note that since the rise of White supremacy there has been no widespread moral indignation on the part of Europeans to their enslavement of Africans and the destruction of millions of our ancestors' human possibilities. The European world has yet to express contrition for its long-standing domination of Africans.

The psychohistorical traditions which gave rise to global White supremacy do not easily allow White supremacists to cease in their anti-African practices. For them to do so is tantamount to the annihilation of their sense of self. Another important consideration is that White supremacy has concomitantly awakened the oppressors to their "buried instincts, to covetousness, violence, race hatred, and moral relativism" (Cesaire, 1972, p. 13). These propensities corrupt the oppressors and arrest their human possibilities. For example, in describing the White Rhodesian soldiers who fought against the Zimbabweans' independence drive, Bruce Moore-King (1988) reasoned: "With every act of brutality, the (White) sons were themselves brutalized. As they became brutalized their acts became more brutal. In the end, none were wholly normal, and many were no longer human" (p. 35). According to a White Rhodesian soldier, "the horror was that in order to 'preserve the standards'...I had to lose my humanity...I never felt emotion again, not anger, not fear, not love, not hate. Nothing" (as reported by Moore-King, 1988, p. 64). Despite the fact that their acts of oppression debase the oppressors, more respected and valued by the White supremacist is the monopoly of power, wealth, and privilege which result from their domination of African people.

As a whole, Europeans refuse to acknowledge and take personal responsibility for the immoral, exploitative character of their racist ideologies and practices. They believe that to admit guilt is to provoke the oppressed to demand that Whites pay reparations. Furthermore the oppressors' consciousness assumes that Africans will, if history permits, extract retribution from them. This White fear phenomenon was recently exhibited by South African Whites. As one of those Whites reported "it's the dred black cloud hanging over us in the future that worries us" (Crapanzano, 1985, p. 233).

This fear of Africans motivates Europeans to persistently strive to strangle our human potentialities. The committed White supremacist must therefore preemptively construe people of African descent as inferior, incapable, and perpetual subjects of White overlordship. These negative stereotypic views of Africans provide the psychological armor for Caucasians to deal with their own psychological insecurities and provide justifications for their oppression of Blacks.

Under universal White supremacy the custodians of apartheid tolerate the existence of Africans only to the extent that Africans cater to the needs of Whites. Similarly, while Africans have been useful in the growth of the West, it has often been stated that we are the White person's burden. In reality, the oppressors view our existence as a threat or encroachment on their divine, natural and historical right to expand. For the White supremacist, our continued existence makes the land barren, our removal makes it broad. As is reported to be said by a South Afrikaner, "the world needs a Hitler in every country"

(Crapanzano, 1985, p. 251). The oppressors' dreams represent our worst fears.

In addition, Europeans entertain the delusional self-image that they are the bringers of ethics and democracy to the world. Europeans rely on words to obscure or change the realities of their persistent, anti-African attitudes, behaviors, ideologies, and practices. For example, Western imperialists defend their behaviors by arguing that the benefits of White overlordship far exceed the negative features. Other Europeans manufacture a veneer of civility and racial fairness that belies their hostile behaviors which maintain White monopoly. In spite of the fact that Africans' quest for self-determination is proscribed by the actions of White supremacists, there is the White view that significant progress has been made in race relations. Lewis (1990) implies that the evils of White supremacy no longer negatively impact the existence of people of African descent and other non-Europeans and that many individuals who champion equality possess "nostalgia for the White man's burden." He writes that "the White man's burden in Kipling's sense—the Westerner's responsibility for the peoples over whom he ruled—has long since been cast off and seized by others...But there are those who still insist on maintaining it—this time as a burden not of power but of guilt, an insistence on responsibility for the world and its ills that is as arrogant and as unjustified as the claims of our imperial predecessors" (Lewis, 1990, p. 102). Nonetheless anti-African practices still pervade the world order. Kovel (1971) writes that, because White racism cannot stand the test of the Europeans' reason nor their better values, Europeans are forced to utilize various mechanisms to defend against the realization of their participation in the racial oppression of people of African descent. It is therefore not uncommon to hear Whites suggest that Caucasians' enslavement of Africans and White racism are simply unfortunate and isolated circumstances. On the other hand, Bobby Wright (1975) insists that "...in their relationship with the black race, Europeans (Whites) are psychopaths and their behavior reflects an underlying biologically transmitted proclivity with roots deep in their evolutionary history" (p. 25). In defense of his general psychopathetic thesis, Wright noted that Whites ignore the concept of morality where race is a variable. He indicated that Whites have a well-established history of denying personal responsibility for the conditions of Africans and that the oppressors show an inability to learn from previous experience.

Throughout this chapter we have argued that, in their relationships with Africans, White supremacists have relied on immoral means to ensure White privilege. This assertion is based on the weight of the psychohistorical evidence. Moreover, one can anticipate no profound moral revolution for Whites to eliminate White supremacy and allow for the natural sharing of the world's resources and power.

The intractable nature of global White supremacy is such that those Whites who attempt to free themselves from involvement in its practice by striving for justice in the world are viewed as anomalies by members of their own group. Moore-King (1988) asserted: "It seems to me that those of my tribe who showed the greatest courage were the very few who said, not that they were right, but that we were wrong. For it is much easier to run with the herd, much easier to pick up a rifle and shoot someone, than it is to endure isolation, the ostracism, the ridicule of your own group" (p. 129).

On the other hand, the oppressed recognize that there are liberal Whites who have not achieved substantial transcendence of their Whiteness. By this we mean that they hold to the illusion of their White superior status and are not fully prepared to see the elimination of White supremacy. Oftentimes, these Whites function to make certain that the response of Blacks to oppression is measured and takes a less radical direction (Biko, 1980).

It is not unusual to hear liberal Whites advising the oppressed to forget the legacy of White supremacy and to adopt 'reasonable' and forgiving attitudes toward the historical White enemy. Another viewpoint is that "liberals are neither permanent friends nor enemies; they are opportunists looking on both sides of any situation, ready to take the side of the issue that suits them best. Their convictions are rarely ever strong and their support is rarely ever consistent" (Clarke, 1991, p. 376).

In light of the global and pervasive nature of White supremacy at the expense of Black humanity, one can safely assume that Europeans will continue to strive for the gratification of their psychohistorical needs for upholding White power, wealth, and prosperity.

Conclusion

People of African descent have historically behaved in ways which suggest to this writer an unawareness of or failure to take seriously the psychohistorical motors of the Europeans' thoughts and actions. Many of our ancestors were overwhelmed by the brutality of White power and their descendants remain victimized. We have indicated that there are differences in worldviews between Africans and Europeans. At the genesis of the Europeans' onslaught of Africans it is quite possible that people of African descent simply did not conceive that universal White supremacy at the expense of African (Black) humanity was possible.

To ensure the liberation of people of African descent we must stand face to face with the psychohistorical testimony of the oppressors' nature. We must proactively deal with the fact that Europeans function on the premise that the relations between groups must always be based upon power and politics, rather than upon ethics. A corollary observation is the historical fact that the great powers of Europe never "retreated to their own ethnic base until they were defeated in a great power war, or (as with Britain after 1945) were so weakened by war that an imperial withdrawal was politically unavoidable" (Kennedy, 1987, p. 514).

We are by no means suggesting that Africans should relinquish their ancestral customs and adopt the oppressors' ways. However for centuries Europeans have viewed our liberation struggle as "rhetoric, disorder, chaos, indicating and commemorating hardship, frustration and anger, impotence and rage, acts of courage and failed courage, hope and despair, loss and death" (Crapanzano, 1985, p. 234). In addition, Africans remain easy prey for the oppressors' tyranny. It is therefore imperative that the African world shore up its power. Several writers have elucidated the psychological and cultural aspects of our liberation struggle (Asante, 1980; Azibo, 1988; Sutherland, 1989), while others have examined the broader political, military, social, and economic questions (Cabral, 1979; Chinweizu, 1975). The prescriptions for liberation invariably point to the need for the oppressed of African descent to engage in daily struggle against those activities which have historically weakened us, such as disunity and disorganized actions against White supremacy, the lack of human resources to engineer development, cooptation by the oppressors, and dependency on Whites.

It is essential that Africans destroy these barriers to liberation and strive for the creation of a world order in which we are liberated and remain liberated. Willpower, tenacity, audacity, lucidity, and the African's resolve to engage in daily struggle against his or her own weaknesses and to struggle against the oppressor will necessarily result in people of African descent recovering greatness, prosperity, wealth, and power. How can the person of African descent make the psychological choice to contribute to our liberation struggle? This question is answered in the next chapter.

Chapter II

THE ROLE OF THE INDIVIDUAL IN THE LIBERATION STRUGGLE

> Where are we going with black nationalism?... We must establish some kind of leadership over ourselves and some kind of discipline among ourselves and some kind of responsibility to ourselves. And I suggest that you start seeking out an ally by finding a mirror.
>
> And you look in that mirror and what's staring back at you until you find your leader, your theoretician, your sage, and your philosopher. Then you start the revolution that will change and put African people on a new road and give them a new destiny.
>
> John Henrik Clarke
Notes For An African World Revolution

Historians have debated the psychological impact of Caucasian tyranny upon Africans. Chancellor Williams (1976) indicated that the critical period in the history of Africans occurred in the years between 1475 and 1675 when European and Asian hordes of barbarians encircled and threatened continental Africans. In commenting on the psychological responses of Africans to these circumstances, Williams hypothesized that a new fatalism emerged which, along with mental atrophy, carried the sentence of ultimate doom to the minds of thousands. He also described the ancient Africans' attempts at personal survival by enslaving and killing their own people. Many Africans were so overwhelmed by European maritime and military capabilities that they thought that the Europeans "must be the Gods of the world" (p. 238). Some Africans thought that the Europeans came to Africa for benevolent purposes, while others decided never to submit to the hostile Caucasoid invaders.

Similarly, discussing the South African context, Allister Sparks (1990) noted that the Dutch peoples' enslavement of the indigenous Xhosa, which began in the early 1600s, engendered certain psychological consequences in these Africans. According to Sparks, "in the end most knuckled under, accepting their state of bondage as best they could and gradually being absorbed into the culture, though never the society. Sometimes years of faithful service could lead to manumission. It bred an attitude of obsequiousness, tinged sometimes with a sarcastic wit and the craftiness of the survivalist, but likely to turn quickly to pleading and grovelling when faced with any threat" (p. 79).

Contemporary Africans display analogous attitudinal and behavioral responses to global White supremacy. Hence, the task of this chapter is to explicate the psychological processes which maintain the oppression of Africans. A critical examination of those personality characteristics, attitudes, and behaviors possessed by various people of African descent which serve to undermine the struggle is a necessary, though not sufficient, condition for collective liberation. Major emphasis, however, will be placed on those psychological properties which must be possessed by people of African descent if we are to emerge victorious in our struggle for liberation.

Existing frameworks focus on colonial (Fanon, 1963), cultural (Semaj, 1981; Nobles, 1986), mental health (Akbar, 1981), and biogenetic concerns (Azibo, 1988) in addressing African persons' responses to oppression. Cultural analysts claim that there exists substantial divergence of cultural practices between Africans and their oppressors. Semaj's (1981) model, for instance, describes the alien who "consistently demonstrates a Eurocentric worldview...and either denigrate or deny their Afrikanity." The diffused person functions to "balance the Black and alien worldviews." The collective, however, "consistently demonstrate an Africentric worldview.... They actively work to build Black institutions, forging cultural, economic, and ultimately, political links" (p. 169-170).

Utilizing a mental health model, Akbar (1981, 1984) considered it insane for African persons to participate in their own oppression. For him, mental health involves African-centeredness, which can only be derived from an affirmation of and commitment to one's African (natural) identity. It also involves engaging in survival and advancement imperatives. Likewise, biogenetic African-centered theories of Black personality (Baldwin, 1981, 1984; Williams, 1981; Azibo, 1988) hold that African-centered constructs, including rhythm, spirituality, communal responsibility, and the essential melanic system, are ontologically rooted in African persons. For biogenetic theorists, the normal-natural African personality "consists of an inhered based in racially biogenetic factors which are imbued with a self (extended and personal) maintenance propensity" (Azibo, 1988, p. 19). Thus, the biogenetic theorists concur with Akbar, but theorize and emphasize the primacy of group—and self-sustentation in natural biogenetic law. Thus, not to engage in self (race) sustentation is insanity or personality disorder for the biogenetic theorists, a deviation from a biogenetically grounded psychological imperative. This author agrees with Akbar's and biogenetic theorists' thesis on correct functioning for African persons. However, I am not totally convinced that the concept of insanity, with its simplicative meanings, is adequate to explain the psychological misorientation of Blacks. While the biogenetic proposition is reasonably compelling, it is difficult to obtain observations of human behavior unaffected by influences of the external world.

The present discussion is informed by the Fanonian principle that we exist in a Manichean world occupied by two different species in perpetual conflict, Europeans and Africans, colonizer and the colonized, oppressors and the oppressed. For centuries, human beings have been born into the legacy, or as Bulhan (1985) argued, "socialized at a tender age in one or the other camp of this world..." (p. 253).

Moreover, we agree when Bulhan further posits that "to live it uncritically and to be outlived by that legacy without taking part in an effort to change it is however a matter of personal choice and responsibility" (p. 253). Hence, for us, the individual's response to that freedom of choice accounts for his or her motivated efforts, the displayed degree of involvement in the struggle for our liberation.

Consistent with the Fanonian principle of a Manichean world, from a personological perspective, African liberation is defined as the psychological functioning of African persons being strongly channeled towards ensuring their nondomination. Subsumed are concerns with our continued survival, the actualizing of our African essence (see Dixon, 1976; Mbiti, 1970; Nobles, 1986), and behaving as the determiners of our destiny. We also agree with Cabral's (1979) definition that "... the struggle is not debate, nor verbiage, whether written or spoken. Struggle is daily action against ourselves (our own weaknesses) and against the enemy" (p. 65).

This chapter takes a phenomenological perspective. It relies heavily on this writer's subjective interpretations of the various orientations and patterns of behavior that people of African descent have displayed in response to their status in the Manichean world. The seminal views of writers on the oppressor-oppressed relationship (Asante, 1980; Fanon, 1963, 1964, 1967; Freire, 1985; Memmi, 1965) are interwoven in this discussion.

The Conceptual Model

Europeans have been the primary architects and perpetrators of a world order in which the African's skin color serves as a stimulus for White tyranny. Various forms of racially inspired violence directed at people of African descent is the norm in societies which are regulated by White supremacy, including Britain, Germany, Russia, China, Ireland, Brazil, the United States, Peru, Canada, and many other countries (Asoyan, 1989; Brooke, 1989; Mydans, 1988; Simmons, 1989). Thus, the present conceptual model has a range of convenience which includes all people of African descent functioning under global White supremacy.

My conceptual model includes four nonideal orientations (the nonstruggler, the reactive struggler, the opportunistic individual, and the partially committed struggler) and an ideal orientation (the authentic struggler). Each orientation delineates global descriptions of observed behavioral regularities in the adult African personality. The regularities result in different stylistic patterns of interpersonal behavior. Focus on adulthood is tied to the notion that this is the period in the life span when the individual is thought to be the agent of his or her own actions. However, in more recent times, we have seen evidence of how a suffocating system of oppression like that in South Africa, can galvanize young people of African descent into struggle. The psychological implications of this phenomenon are to be determined. The four nonideal orientations are typified by the attitudes, personality attributes, and behavioral patterns that are antithetical to our collective liberation. The authentic style is conceived of as the ideal orientation which will serve to facilitate the liberation of people of color.

It should be noted that these orientations are not hierarchic developmental stages, but rather orthogonal dimensions. Conceptually, the model allows for transition from the nonideal orientation to the ideal one. However, to be an authentic struggler is to make the irreversible decision to struggle for our liberation. Another importantly salient point is that no gender and class distinctions are associated with the orientations.

Racial Socialization

The precise processes which create the above cited orientations are unclear. Specifically, as it deals with theorizing on the ideal orientation, early racial socialization is postulated to be essential. Positive role models, like parents and/or members of the extended African community, are significant in the struggle for liberation. The beliefs, affects, and behaviors of these adults reflect liberating praxis.

These role models infuse in African youth a love for and commitment to African people. They share the stories of African resistance and teach of the weaknesses of our ancestors that resulted in the enslavement and colonization of our people. These role models also discuss the continuing need for struggle against the oppressors and impart to Black youth their moral obligation to ensure the survival and advancement of the African world. Instilling pride in African ancestry and encouraging the development of psychological Africanity could account for the development of the authentic struggler. Yet, ultimately the authentic being evolves from the individual's sustained will and intent to struggle for our liberation.

Concerning the development of the nonideal orientation, especially problematic are research findings on Black children's preference for White culture (Clark and Clark, 1947; Spencer,

1984; Spencer and Horowitz, 1973). This antiself bias is quite common in the African world. In the profoundly racist countries, African youth experience crises of racial and cultural identity which lead them to display racially dysfunctional behaviors. One major reason for these phenomena is that Black parents are failing, for the most part, to encourage the development of ethnic consciousness and to deal explicitly with concerns of the Black community. Information on the culture and history of people of African descent concerning our common oppression and the need for collective struggle to ensure our liberation is not being transmitted to African youth during their early and critical developmental years.

Some parents who are aware of these concerns incorrectly argue that to expose our youth to such racial matters only serves to make them vulnerable to White hostility. Ignoring the notion that racial socialization can lead to the development of a Pan-African consciousness and self-determination in African youth, another parental argument is that racial discussions may lead their offsprings to be racists, that is, to hate White people. Spencer (1984) reported that African-American parents' child-rearing practices emphasized generic human values. She noted that their humanistic approach leaves Black children essentially unprepared to handle the demands of the Manichean world.

Parents can stress both the exclusive concerns of the oppressed of African descent and propagate the principle of universal benevolence (Stuckey, 1987). African parents ought to impart to their children the necessity of working for the upliftment and advancement of Africans because we continue to experience the inimical consequences of the enslavement epoch, subsequent colonization, and perpetual domination of Europeans and other non-African races. In short, our children must be consistently instructed that there is no humanity before that which starts with the African self (Garvey, 1967).

It is also this author's belief that Black parents should be prepared to share with their children insightful analysis concerning the rise of White supremacy. For example African youth must be told that the testimony of history is that the anti-African violence of Europeans can be traced to these peoples' uninhibited expressions of their ancestral customs within the context of the African world. Parents of African descent ought to develop an understanding in African youth that the maleficent cultural traditions of Europeans including their expansionistic, materialistic, military, Napoleonic, segregating, and warlike propensities have instigated and maintained White tyranny against African peoples. This perspective does not in any way advocate anti-White sentiments in Africans. It stresses instead that people of African descent must work towards the creation of a new world order within which Africans can become liberated and stay liberated.

Indeed White youth are tacitly and blatantly socialized to uphold White power, wealth, sovereignty, and prosperity. Black parents, in contrast, have socialized their children to survive White hostility. We recognize the well-intentioned motives of parents to shelter their children from palpable White racism. Yet internalization of these parental attitudes by African children has typically resulted in an African adult who is accommodating to White supremacy. Black parents should communicate to their offspring that each African person's cardinal interest must be the dignity, prosperity, survival, and sovereignty of the African race.

Individual Differences in Response to the Struggle

The following conceptual model elucidates essential personological considerations toward the liberation of people of African descent. The details of the determining historical and contemporary societal influences on the development of the various stylistic patternings of behaving is outside this chapter's focus.

It should be noted that there is no intent to suggest that any given individual will fit neatly into one category. One goal of this chapter, however, is to further the understanding of the psychological processes which allow for Africans to participate in either their oppression or our quest for collective liberation. The intent is to facilitate the positive development and advancement of people of African descent.

The Nonstruggler

This individual's psychological functioning is directed toward the maximization of his or her personal survival. The determinants of this goal include, but are not limited to, inadequate early racial socialization, cold complicity with the oppressor, and the individual's cognitions reflecting miseducation or information deficits on both the Manichean condition and the liberation process. On the affective level, individuals may experience fear, distress, fatigue, anxiety, depression, frustration, indifference, disillusionment, and other negative affects from having previously waged unsuccessful methods of struggle against European oppression. Given the thesis of the oppressed status of people of color, however, individual and group consequences are associated with the aim of personal survival.

On the individual level defensive functioning finds expression in the nonstruggler's personality structure. Hence the presence of defenses indicates the personal conflicts and confusion which nonstrugglers experience in handling the Manichean condition. A plausible hypothesis is that the psyche of African people has lodged within it an awareness of the Manichean world's design. One contention is that nonstrugglers institute defenses to avoid possible feelings of guilt, impotence, or anxiety which might accompany their failure to lend support to the collective struggle. On the other hand, nonstrugglers have developed defense mechanisms that conceal their "innermost thought and present an image that they expect the White baas expects and wants to see" (Sparks, 1990, p. 214).

Rationalization is one prominent defense. For example, to defend their removal from the collective struggle, nonstrugglers

The Role of the Individual in the Liberation Struggle 45

often seek to invalidate the need for struggle. Hence it is common to hear these persons insist that the question of struggle is moot given that existing conditions suggest no successful outcomes. A corollary observation is that nonstrugglers construe African liberation as romanticism and take European supremacy for granted. Fanon (1963) saw such individuals "as beaten from the start" (p. 63). According to him, "there is no need to demonstrate their incapacity to triumph...They take it for granted in everyday life and political maneuvers" (p. 63).

For Bobby Wright (1975), one form of rationalization was the tendency of "some individuals to fantasize that Blacks have reached their destiny and attempt to act accordingly as free men" (p. 31). However, as I will demonstrate throughout this book, Africans are not independent with respect to important human activities such as economic, political, psychological, cultural, and military considerations. So, as Chinweizu (1975) advises, "we must wipe from our eyes all delusions of freedom if we are to see clearly our way to real freedom" (p. 497).

An additional conspicuous psychological feature of nonstrugglers is that they function as receptive beings. These individuals expect to receive satisfaction of psychological and material needs from the oppressor. Thus they remain objects for the oppressor. Erich Fromm (1941) noted that this receptive orientation develops in a society that fosters the exploitation of one group by another. One behavioral outcome observed to be associated with this receptive orientation is that nonstrugglers tend to consistently downplay, if not out right deny, the negative effects of blatant and subtle acts of oppression on people of color. In several instances nonstrugglers will attribute the oppressed status to our personal (i.e., apathy and failure to assimilate European values) and culturally rooted maladjustments (i.e., drug use and violence in the Black community).

Another prominent feature of nonstrugglers is their reliance on "magical explanations or a false view of God, to whom they fatalistically transfer the responsibility for their oppressed state" (Freire, 1985, p. 163). Specifically, there are those Blacks, even supposedly educated ones, who insist that people of African descent are cursed by God. This, according to them, explains why Blacks have so many difficulties. Freire (1985) observed that "it is extremely unlikely that these self-mistrustful, downtrodden, hopeless people will seek their own liberation—an act of rebellion which they may view as a disobedient violation of the will of God, as an unwarranted confrontation with destiny" (p. 163).

These nonideal persons also insist that the oppressed of African descent suffer from color phobia. The assumption is that Africans are so caught up in their victimized status that they have developed a "victim-focused identity" and preemptively construe their experiences strictly in terms of White racism. For some observers, this victim-focused identity is one chief reason why people of African descent are unwilling to take responsibility for improving themselves and the Black community and are so eager to blame Whites for their own failings. Shelby Steele (1990) noted that people of African descent ignore their real fears of racial inferiority and cling to an adversarial and victim-focused identity to provoke White guilt. According to him, Blacks derive a sense of power from these behaviors. There is also the suggestion from Goodman (1990) "that no doubt there are Blacks who get a kick out of any attack on Whites and cry amen to any pipe dream of salvation" (p. 22).

We certainly agree that African people must demonstrate greater self-reliance and self-determination in improving the Black condition. Yet these commentators overlook the fact that African persons are victims of the actions of committed White supremacists. Their arguments also fail to acknowledge White society's need to perpetuate a system that victimizes people of color.

In sum, we contend that these nonideal persons' arguments may be related to the operation of defense mechanisms geared toward avoiding punishments and receiving rewards from the oppressor. They may, as Fuller (1984) contended, "prefer to look away from the racists so that they will not be forced to face their lack of power as compared to the power of the racists. They prefer to look at each other" (p. 16).

In a related vein, the social psychological literature on individual mobility indicates that individuals may try to move from a lower to a higher status group by disassociating themselves from their original group (Jahoda, 1961; Klineberg and Zavalloni, 1969). Nonstrugglers who seek upward mobility appear to function as if success in the Manichean world is best achieved by adopting the oppressor's criterion for achievement and therefore striving to resemble to oppressor (Memmi, 1965). Or, as Fanon (1967) informed us, these nonstrugglers have "only one destiny. And it is to be White." Attempts at deracination are believed to be the result of the African person's need to compensate for feelings of racial inferiority.

Another salient consideration relates to the convincing evidence that the affective or feeling mode is a notable aspect of the psychology of African people (Brown and Forde, 1950; Dixon, 1976; Elan, 1968; Levine, 1974). Yet, an interesting feature of the psychological reality of some nonstrugglers is their propensity to view emotional responses to oppression as inappropriate behavior. The nonstrugglers' outrage against their own degradation is repressed, suppressed, or eliminated through protracted compromise and failure to boldly confront the oppressor. If oppression is to be addressed at all, this group argues for the adoption of cold and calculating reasoning. However they rarely employ such an approach out of "fear to confront institutionalized violence and internalized prohibitions" (Freire, 1985, p. 260).

It should be noted that the nonstruggler's aim of personal survival leads to certain group consequences. Bulhan (1985) posited that this "leaves the oppressed defenseless, divided, and highly prone to capitulation. The aim of personal salvation when one's group is oppressed is often a chimera and, if attained, involves one or another form of alienation and sometimes even outright self and/or collective betrayal" (p. 258). Moreover, Chinweizu (1975) indicated that "a western individualist ethos weakens the person's African identity, destroys that person's commitment to an African communalist ethos, and erases the individual's sense of patriotic responsibility to Africa" (p. 76-77). In brief, nonstrugglers have transferred their loyalties from their genetic communities to those of their conquerors and have lost their ability to define themselves (Chinweizu, 1975).

The Reactive Struggler

The reactive struggler possesses a personality structure devoid of certain attributes including courage, decisiveness, feelings of worth, and clarity of self. S(he) is unable to direct proactive efforts toward liberation. Furthermore, similar to the nonstruggler, the reactive struggler lacks the African sense of a collective or extended self (Nobles, 1986). One contention is that this individual would remain a nonstruggler if s(he) were not so offended by an accumulated sense of experienced victimization at the hands of the oppressor. This provides the catalyst for the reactive individual's involvement in the struggle. The reactive struggler appears incapable of struggling on an individual level and instead struggles as part of a group effort. Thus oppression is experienced at the individual level, but reaction is strictly through a group effort. As mentioned earlier, collective and interdependent functioning is purported to be a primary aspect of the psychology of African people. However, in the case of the reactive struggler, involvement at the group level is not representative of a sense of mutual responsibility but rather serves self-interests which are orthogonal to the collective goal of liberation.

The reactive struggler takes part in a collective effort out of a deep fear of being identified or singled out by the oppressor. In addition to gaining anonymity, collective effort allows for diffusion of responsibility. The reactive struggler's personality appears to require shielding from the oppressor's hostile attempts to subvert African peoples' acts of self-determination. Although the group acts as a potential shield, this individual remains consistently vulnerable to the oppressor's ways. When exposed to the atmosphere of violence generated by the oppressor, feelings of powerlessness, demoralization, and psychophysiological arousal elicit attempts by the reactive person to withdraw from the struggle. To defend this decision, arguments may be forwarded on the interpersonal problems experienced in the group. On the other hand, the oppressor's pacification methods (e.g., economic rewards and verbal appeasements) can also smooth the reactive struggler's wounds of oppression.

In these and other instances it is evident that the consciousness of nonideal persons is controllable by the overt and unsuspecting means of the oppressor. One can conjecture that the nonideal person would even distrust his or her own conceptual understanding, bodily wisdom, or intuitive sense of an event, if the oppressor were to present an alternative viewpoint. Here the oppressed negates the essential premise that the greater the differences between the philosophical, psychological, cultural, social, and other human activities of the dominated people and those of the oppressors, the more assured the victory of liberation (Cabral, 1979).

Reactive persons also supplant negative responses to the White supremacist with politeness. When the reactive struggler feels particularly conspicuous in the presence of the oppressor there is the tendency for the reactive individual to display a cultivated civility which masks this person's true feelings of fear, hostility, and anger toward the oppressor. This results in the reactive person's accommodating to the oppressive racial status quo.

In conjunction, like the nonstruggler, the reactive person has a tendency to insist on the nonexistent possibilities for the removal and destruction of our oppression. One possible reason for these behaviors is that the reactive struggler becomes involved in struggle to seek psychic relief from a sense of personal victimization. Yet, at some point in time, this person learns that the "question of oppression is primarily a problem of psyches confronting each other" (Bulhan, 1985, p. 118). The reactive struggler does not possess the requisite personality attributes to withstand such confrontations and has yet to see that struggle can harden one's courage (Sartre, 1968).

Both the nonstruggler and reactive individual do not have a historical sense and appreciation for the struggles of African peoples. Neither exhibits a profound nor lasting commitment to the liberation of people of African descent. Indeed, in the case of the reactive struggler, if personal relief from oppression occurs, however temporary, or if the group disbands, the struggle has ended for this person. However, the current conceptualization does hold that reactive persons remain candidates for involvement in the struggle, along the lines described, if they continue to be offended by the oppressors' acts of victimization. The important point is that the reactive struggler is somewhat able to struggle against oppression, but has not reached the higher level where s(he) can struggle for liberation. In *Afrocentricity* Molefi Asante cautions that "struggle itself turns into oppressive consciousness when one cannot conceive of victory (p. 58).

The reactive struggler, like the nonstruggler, possesses a receptive orientation and expects to find the "source of all good" in the oppressor. One concomitant of this is that the receptive being adheres to a "child-like" faith in the malleability of the oppressors' attitudes and behaviors. They also yearn for peaceful coexistence with the oppressor on terms defined by the oppressor. These Blacks do not fully understand that there can be no reconciliation between oppressors and those who they oppress, between masters and those who serve them. As a consequence, these reactive individuals do not recognize that to "transform a situation of oppression requires at once a relentless confrontation of oppressors without, who are impervious to appeals of reason and compassion, and an equally determined confrontation of the oppressor within...For without the dual confrontation, the search for personal harmony remains illusive..." (Bulhan, 1985, p. 277).

A major distinction between the reactive struggler and the nonstruggler is that the former will focus on the victimization and exploitation of African peoples, while, for the most part, this will be absent from the latter's communications. Analysis of the reactive struggler's concern reveals that the defense mechanism of projection is being used to protect this individual's fragile sense of self. The reactive struggler postulates that s(he) does not personally possess any objectionable qualities that cause his or her victimization; rather, it is inherent in the oppressor's nature to denigrate and victimize people of color.

There is truth to the reactive individual's reasoning. However, for self-empowerment to occur, it is necessary for this person to accept responsibility for his or her weaknesses and limitations. In addition, the historical records suggest that when the oppressed accept the absolute consequences associated with struggle, including physical death, they begin to possess a true passion for an existence without oppression (Fanon, 1963).

The Opportunistic Individual

In contrast to the two previously discussed orientations, at first glance the opportunistic individual appears to be committed to our collective liberation. This, however, is not the case, because this individual espouses a liberation ideology which is not coterminous with his or her behavior. This incongruence culminates in a lifestyle that is inconsistent with struggle, and in several instances can prove inimical to the collective interests of people of color.

It should be emphasized that the perceived incongruity between attitude and behavior is argued to be the result of a process whereby the opportunistic person exploits a liberation ideology in an attempt to manufacture a public persona. It is the person's belief that the donning of this mask will allow for the satisfaction of various deficiency needs, including the need for esteem, grandeur, recognition, power, or money. It would seem to this writer that if an individual is primarily motivated to seek the satisfaction of personal deficiency needs, then the collective struggle may be of secondary concern, and in the extreme instance, of no concern at all.

It is further posited that the opportunistic individual's deficiency needs are derived from real or imagined feelings of inferiority. We argue that in this Manichean world, these feelings have their genesis in the opportunistic person's perceptions of their powerlessness and the decimation of their humanity. Opportunistic persons have not, however, learned to solve the problem of oppression in a psychological and politically useful way. Indeed, whatever aggressiveness is directed toward the oppressor functions in the opportunistic person's self-interests. Furthermore, we accept Fanon's (1963) argument that an oppressed person who functions opportunistically "has clothed this aggressiveness in his barely veiled desire to assimilate himself to the colonial world." It is also typical of some opportunistic persons to experience personal anguish when the oppressor fails to respond favorably to their attempts to achieve the privileges of the racially oppressive environment.

The opportunistic person has a variety of avenues available for the satisfaction of deficiency needs. Temporal and situational considerations may determine the choice of a liberation ideology. To illustrate, an individual may challenge a racist institution and appear to be a struggler against our oppression. The opportunistic person however believes that challenging the system will allow for some satisfaction of the central deficiency need. At the same time this individual recognizes that to be taken seriously by members of one's own African ethnic group as well as by racially dissimilar individuals, one must appear to be knowledgeable about their subject matter. Hence they utilize Africentric attitudes and words. Because such Africentricity finds no true resonance in this individual's personality structure, one observes painful contradictions in psychological functioning.

It is certainly not surprising when one finds opportunistic persons who have a paucity of knowledge on and care even less about the struggles of African peoples. These opportunistic individuals are contextually and temporally limited, guided by deficiency needs, and fail to show solidarity with people of African descent. To the degree to which the satisfaction of deficiency needs remains the primary motivation of opportunistic persons, they will not be true advocates for maximum self-determination. Opportunistic persons, especially those who purport to be our leaders, pose serious problems for the African community. Among other things they are incapable of genuine political mobilization to deal with the exigencies of the Manichean world, that is, European cultural imperialism, introoppression (the internalization of the oppressor without), and autooppression (the destructive behaviors directed by people of color against each other) (Bulhan, 1985). Instead, opportunistic leaders foster mistrust, factionalism, and are easily coopted by the oppressor. Opportunistic leaders who are governed by deficiency needs such as the myth of their own grandeur have historically proven to be serious threats to the liberation struggle. Writing on continental Africans, Chinweizu (1975) observed that opportunistic leaders are not concerned with the liberation of the whole society from imperial relations, but they have been historically contented to "seek those civil liberties that would enable them to inherit colonial privileges and attain "civilized" status. He wrote that "once opportunistic leaders have achieved what power they sought, they quickly abandoned the masses to disillusion..." (p. 96).

Similar outcomes can be observed in Blacks throughout the diaspora. For instance, there have been several reports of former Black Panther leaders in the United States who traded African nationalism rhetoric for personal ambition in White political structures (Johnson, 1990). Clearly these individuals have found what they consider to be a favorable environmental context for the fulfillment of their primary wish to gain personal rewards from a racially oppressive structure.

One reason why opportunistic leaders remain in our community is because of the long-standing reluctance of people of African descent to hold these purported leaders accountable. This fact is further complicated by the opportunistic person's rhetoric which tends to have a cathartic effect on the oppressed masses. S(he) articulates the sufferings and hopes of a long oppressed people and propagandizes that the conditions of the oppressed are solely attributable to the actions of Europeans. Most importantly, perhaps, the opportunistic leader deceives the masses into believing that the salvation of the oppressed will be assured by the concessions of the oppressors.

Oftentimes the opportunistic leader will ignore the dysfunctional individual and community behaviors which allow for African persons to participate in their oppression. Hence the opportunistic person's rhetoric tends to remove the onus from the oppressed to control their own destiny. The opportunistic person neither seeks for the elimination of Africans' inferior status nor for us to be self-determining and independent in world affairs.

In sum, similar to the other nonideal orientations, the opportunistic individual does not appear to perceive that "a collective drama will never be settled through individual solutions" (Memmi, 1965, p. 126). The opportunistic person has not internalized the fact that there can be no authentic individual freedom in the absence of the collective liberation of people of African descent.

The Partially Committed Struggler

The partially committed orientation represents the closest approximation to the ideal orientation. The person possessing this orientation has some appreciation for the historical and contemporary effects of racism, colonialism, and oppression on people of color. This enables the partially committed person to display proactive and self-directed actions toward our liberation. However, at the same time this person is partially committed to the struggle because s(he) is not fully prepared to accept the absolute consequences associated with struggle. The fundamental explanation for this observation is that the partially committed individual is integrating Africentric thoughts, attitudes, and behaviors. This process is often rife with conflict because the partially committed individual is attempting to straddle two cultures—the European and the African. By necessity, such a person "is rarely well-seated, and the colonized does not always find the right pose" (Memmi, 1965, p. 124).

This process has been variously described as double consciousness (Du Bois, 1904), diffused (Semaj, 1981), or biculturality (Chimezie, 1985). Discussions on this topic point invariably to the inherent psychological conflicts associated with having to relate to the contradictory expectations of two cultures. Writing on the African-American situation, Du Bois (1904) noted: "One ever feels this twoness—an American, a negro; two souls, two thoughts, two unreconciled strivings, two warring ideals in one dark body" (p. 15). In a similar train of thought, Sterling Plumpp (1987) contended that for "Black Americans to survive in the United States means a preoccupation with systematically learning all the skills necessary for survival; this means becoming whatever it means to be an 'American' on the surface but keeping our commitment to Black people as the first priority" (p. 79-80).

There are various propositions on the development of double consciousness in people of color, with European oppression noted as the primary source (Chimezie, 1985). As it relates to this discussion, this bifurcation in functioning does not allow for a strong liberation consciousness to develop and energize behavior. The partially committed person does not fully embrace the thesis that oppressors, by definition, intend to undermine the humanity of the oppressed and to maintain the status quo of oppression. To illustrate, there are those partially committed persons who possess a dread of the Europeans' adverse opinions and actions. Hence, while working in a racist setting, these individuals will over extend themselves so that the oppressor can observe. It is their hope that the oppressor will appreciate and reward this industriousness. Still other partially committed individuals have suggested that they want to show competence on a task so that "White people won't say that because I am Black, I can't do anything." Yet, "trying to fight our condition with proofs that confine our efforts to peripheral activities is like trying to exorcise an evil with conjuring tricks" (Chinweizu, 1975, p. 397).

Evidently the partially committed strugglers' personality structure contains remnants of a colonized mentality which allows this person to seek validation from his or her oppressors. The quest of nonideal persons for White approval naturally results in the adhesion of the oppressed to the oppressors (Freire, 1985).

In brief, the person possessing the partially committed orientation is unaccepting of the idea that the oppressor's views of the oppressed are often impervious to experience; behavior which is inconsistent with the oppressor's belief system may not be seen at all. Furthermore, the testimony of history is that the oppressor "listens to nothing but his fears, greed and mistaken beliefs" (Mathabane, 1986, p. 255). Thus, as the oppressor capitulates, s(he) never becomes converted (Fanon, 1963).

There are several consequences associated with the partially committed person's reliance on the oppressor as a source for his or her self-validation. In the absence of a mature African liberation consciousness, intermittent concessions from the oppressor can confuse this person's perceptions about the nature of the oppressor. On the other hand persistent exposure to the uninhibited anti-African hostility of the oppressor could powerfully provoke the partially committed struggler to realize the unfairness of such treatment. Critical self-analysis may reveal the fallacy of anticipating self-approval from the perennial enemies of people of African descent.

Because of the veracity, however tenuous, of the partially committed person's position on our liberation, coupled with a minimum of defensiveness, a transformation to total commitment to the struggle is possible. This will require rejecting the challenge of assimilation; as long as the Black person is among his or her own, this diminishes the opportunities for the oppressed to experience their being through the oppressors' (Fanon, 1963).

Similarly, for transformation to authenticity, it is vitally important for nonideal persons to function more in accordance with Africentric consciousness. This will allow for a greater clarity and integrity of self; concomitantly a collective consciousness will become transcendental to the personal ego.

A finer grain analysis is possible within each nonideal orientation. For example, subsumed are those individuals of color who are predators on their own community, such as pimps, drug pushers, the perpetrators of Black-on-Black crime, the unconcerned Black middle class, and so on. While we cannot elaborate on these issues in this chapter, it should be emphasized that these individuals function to undermine the struggle for liberation.

Pertaining to the unconcerned middle class persons of African descent, this group has been variously defined in terms of its cultural lethargy, passivity, and ideological submissiveness to White supremacy (Cruse, 1967; Fanon, 1963; Frazier, 1973). The Black elite has a long tradition of serving the interests of the oppressors and ignoring the common plight of Africans. They deny or reject the collective concerns of the African community and have invariably allied themselves with Europeans to obtain and preserve their short term personal gains. The tendency of the Black elite is to relinquish their membership in the African race for ephemeral acceptance from Whites. Similar to other nonideal persons, the Black elite is convinced of the racial inferiority of people of African descent. Hence, these Blacks believe that to achieve social parity with Whites, they must reject their Africanity and identify with Europeans.

Another prominent habit of the deracinated Black elite is to complain that it is racist for Blacks to insist on the primacy of their own interests. They also find it racist for Blacks to insist on being the primary and sole agents of their political, economic, military, and national affairs. Yet these dysfunctional Blacks never openly deplore the fact that White Americans, White Germans, White Britons, and so forth, are the primary authors of their national and political destiny. In short, the Black elite will continue to serve the oppressors' interests in order to preserve their personal success. Consequently the African liberation struggle is of no relevance to this group.

In sum the nonstruggler, reactive, opportunistic, and partially committed individuals all experience self-doubt. They all hold some degree of admiration for the oppressor and adhere to the view that the "almighty power of the colonizer might bear the fruit of infinite goodness" (Memmi, 1965, p. 127). Thus no tenacity is brought to bear on our liberation struggle. In some form or another, capitulation to the forces of oppression has occurred.

Furthermore nonideal persons' preoccupation with their own physical and psychological survival exceeds their desire for our collective liberty. These individuals, having "become alienated beings for another...are not able to develop authentically. Deprived of their own power of decision, which is located in the oppressor, they follow the prescriptions of the latter. The oppressed only begin to develop when, surmounting the contradictions in which they are caught, they become beings for themselves" (Freire, 1985, p. 160).

The Authentic Struggler

The authentic struggler accepts that the liberation of the oppressed is facilitated when, at the individual level, the person of African descent sees value in self. Thus the authentic struggler is dedicated to his or her African self and by extension to all African persons. Behavioral manifestations of this level of dedication involves not allowing the oppressor to manipulate him or her to maintain the oppression of people of African descent. The authentic struggler lives in accordance with African-centered attitudes, and places great value on the interconnectedness of African people.

The authentic struggler is a person of culture. This person functions on the assumption that African cultural realities of unity, reciprocity, and respect for the sacredness of Black existence are critical in the struggle for liberation. The consciousness of authentic strugglers is informed by our collective history and common concern. In brief this ideal struggler has fallen in love

The Role of the Individual in the Liberation Struggle

with the race and consistently sacrifices for our uplift (Woodson, 1933).

Authentic strugglers are convinced that a situation of oppression can never be adjusted to. Such persons "take it for granted that existing in the biological sense of the word and existing as a sovereign people are synonymous" (Fanon, 1964, p. 78). They also take as truth that "if we have any pride, any dignity, any distaste for the physical, mental, and moral pains of abasement, our only stake in the present order of things would be to change it" (Chinweizu, 1975, p. 483). For authentic strugglers, the fundamental fact of life, the directionality of life, includes not only our continuation and advancement but also the assurance that we, the people of African descent, become the real determiners of our destiny. Authentic strugglers do not simply seek justice, but strive for the liberation of productive forces and the enhancement of African persons' psychological, military, economic, cultural, social, spiritual, and political progress.

The authentic strugglers, showing none of the defensiveness of the nonideal individuals, possess a true and lucid consciousness of the Manichean world's design. They perceive clearly the attitudes and behaviors, that is, arrogance, moral blindness, and contempt for the oppressed, that accompany the oppressors' "will to rule." At the same time this consciousness is accompanied by the authentic beings' acceptance of the risks and responsibilities associated with the liberation struggle.

The proactive and self-directed behavior of authentic strugglers depict a higher-order level of psychological and political behavior. Oppressors are unable to predict these individuals' actions and show concern about the possibilities evident in authentic strugglers. The historical records show that this has led to grave acts of persecution of our more public authentic strugglers, including Marcus Garvey, Queen Nzingha, Yaa Asantewa, Toussaint L'Ouverture, Steve Biko, Malcolm X, and Patrice Lumumba. Yet, it is argued that oppressors are incapable of destroying the authentic person's solid cultural, psychological, and political commitment to our struggle. The authentic struggler has achieved a firm integration of Africentric attitudes, traits, and behaviors. The oppressors' ways cannot impact such wholeness of being.

The struggle is the authentic individual's life. As Marcus Garvey stated, "I live and die for Africa redeemed ... and the day that I forsake my people may God almighty say 'there shall be no more light for you' (Martin, 1983, p. 114 & 221). Similarly Cabral (1979) wrote, "so far as we are able to think of our common problem, the problems of our people, of our own folk, putting in their right place our personal problems, and, if necessary, sacrificing our personal interests we can achieve miracles" (p. 75).

Authentic strugglers show compliance with their will to freedom, a will which exceeds any of their psychological and physical fears. According to Steve Biko (1980), "If you can overcome the personal fear of death, which is a highly irrational thing, you know that you are on your way" (p. 152). Similarly Patrice Lumumba (1978) stated that "it is not I myself who count. It is the Congo...Neither brutality, nor cruelty, nor torture will ever bring me to ask for mercy, for I prefer to die with my head unbowed, my faith unshakable and with profound trust in the destiny of my country, rather than live under subjection and disregarding sacred principles...Long Live Africa" (p. 15-16).

The possessors of the authentic style have historically been the ones with the human spirit which accounts for the survival of the African community. In the two hundred year period between 1475 and 1675 within which Africans were hemmed in and threatened in all directions by European and Asian predators, Chancellor Williams (1976) argues there were those African ancestors who "resolved never to yield, to move and keep on moving rather than submit, to rebuild...and to fight for unity as the only route to survival" (Williams, 1976, p. 238) and the liberation of our people. Collective liberation, then, requires an exponential increase of individuals displaying the authentic lifestyle.

Transition from Nonideal to Authentic Functioning

The processes which precipitate the development of the authentic lifestyle in adulthood are contended to be quite complex. At the more general level, as previously noted, in the final analysis each person chooses to become an authentic struggler. It is worth repeating the role that early developmental processes can play in facilitating the authentic lifestyle. The African child must be made to feel worthy, secure, and strong. S(he) must learn to respect and love African persons and culture. African youth must internalize the information on our common oppression and the quest for liberation. Without adequate love, security, feelings of esteem and worthiness, and knowledge of the African condition it is difficult to grow in adulthood to the point of authenticity.

Furthermore, for collective liberation to have deep significance, it demands nonideal persons realizing and accepting the roles that their weaknesses, fears, individualistic strivings, defenses, and other dysfunctional behaviors, attitudes, and affects play in maintaining the Manichean condition. One suggestion is that these persons seek ways to relinquish such personality dynamics. It is vitally important for nonideal persons to excavate these negative attributes from their psychological existence. They must localize the oppressor outside of themselves (Freire, 1985). Only in this way will the oppressed develop the uncompromising determination to contribute to the construction of a new world order in which people of African descent will become liberated and stay liberated.

In addition, reclamation of African cultural and behavioral patterns is essential. The oppressed should immerse themselves in the literature of those Black scholars who have described the ways in which Blacks deviate from their core African identity (Asante, 1980; Baldwin, 1987; Fanon, 1967). Most significantly this literature provides important and useful recommendations for self-transformation to authenticity. To illustrate, in dealing with the need for Africans to be resocialized to their own cultural traditions, Asante (1980) emphasized the importance of constructing and changing "concepts of symbols so that they become more consistent with the Afrocentric point of view." He also spoke of enabling, which involves "managing the breakdown of the old order so that dependent needs are met and filled by people becoming more self-reliant," and liberating, which involves developing "alternative lifestyles and relationships and the use of Afrocentricity to secure freedom" (p. 103).

I must emphasize here that Black peoples' knowledge of their liberation literature and the historical literature on their long-standing enemies will most likely lead to the development of psychological and political maturity. Such maturity will serve as an effective barrier against the oppressors' attempts to manipulate the oppressed for their own benefits. Finally, the development of racial pride and dignity as well as a liberation consciousness is required for these persons of African descent to realize that self-empowerment and activism of the oppressed lead to liberation.

Conclusion

I have attempted to explore the bases for improvement in the psychological functioning of people of African descent. To that end I have elucidated the psychological features of ideal functioning. Explorations of the personal and environmental factors that cultivate and maintain the authentic struggler's "will to collective liberation" are needed. These will provide information which can be translated into prescriptions for the development of the ideal orientation.

In sum this chapter has argued that oppression remains a prepotent force in the lives of people of African descent, and that African peoples' stylistic patterns of behaving play some role in both the maintenance of our oppression, and our quest toward collective liberation. Our noted historian, Dr. John Henrik Clarke insisted that the struggle is first and foremost a psychological one with political, spiritual, economic, educational, social, and other implications. He contended that African people can not save and liberate themselves until they first love themselves. The development and maintenance of the authentic lifestyle must be the life-goal of the African person.

Chapter III

THE MARGINALIZATION OF THE AFRICAN WORLD

> *Not until the Black man strikes out independently to do for himself and proves his nettle in nation building, commerce, industry, politics and war, will he be rated as one of the forces of the world.*
>
> Marcus Garvey

Introduction

Africa, the mother of human civilization, has made profound and significant contributions to human development and progress. The literature is replete with examples on the inventions of Africans that enabled human survival and progress (Clarke, 1971; Jackson, 1970; Ki-Zerbo, 1981). In conjunction, Africans played a major role in the formulative development of philosophical, political, and religious thoughts from which world civilization has benefitted. Akhenaton, an African pharaoh, is credited with introducing the belief in one God (monotheism), to humanity. Plato, Aristotle, and Euclid all spent time in Egypt studying under the ancient Egyptian priests (Bernal, 1987; Jackson, 1970). Ivan Van Sertima (1976, 1987) has presented evidence on the early travels of ancient Africans to Asia, Europe, China, Japan, Turkey, and to the Americas.

The European enslavement of Africans, which began in the 1440s and reached its culmination in the 1880s, has generated an increase in discussion on the plight of Africans. The goal of this chapter is to present an assessment of how people of African descent are faring both in Africa and in the diaspora. Interwoven in this discussion are the historical and current variables which have functioned to marginalize the African world and undermine the liberation of people of African descent.

This chapter describes how the transatlantic enslavement trade, colonial rule, and contemporary factors resulted in the social, economic, health, industrial, military, and technological difficulties faced by people of African descent.

As was suggested in the previous chapters, and to be further explored in this and subsequent chapters, people of African descent have developed various dysfunctional attitudes and behaviors in response to their marginalized status in a world controlled by White supremacy. As a result, African liberation, defined as the psychological functioning of African persons strongly channeled towards their nondomination, is of no concern to many people of African descent.

The present discussion is based on the premise that the marginality of the African world has allowed various White cultural groups to traditionally regard people of African descent as inferiors and undeserving of equal treatment. The subsequent chapter will demonstrate how instinctive racist attitudes and practices, which are particularly palpable and virulent in the West, have operated to undermine and destroy the life opportunities and self-determination of people of African descent. It is critical for people of African descent to understand the nature and range of their oppressive experiences in order to resolve and transcend these forces and deal more earnestly with the question of the collective struggle. It is important, therefore, to reiterate that Africans must harbor in their awareness the fact that they have a moral responsibility to eradicate the victimization of Africans and contribute to the struggle for our collective liberation.

Historical and Colonial Background

There is an exhaustive literature on the enslavement and colonial experiences of Africans therefore I will not attempt to discuss these situations in great detail. Nevertheless I am convinced that some of these details must be highlighted in order to gain understanding of their spillover effects on the contemporary experiences of Africans.

As indicated in a previous chapter, Africa, of all the continents, has been the one whose destiny has been most conditioned by hostile foreign influences. Historical evidence suggests that this process started about 1675 B.C. when the Asian hordes of barbarians, the Hyksos, invaded and occupied lower Egypt. The Hyksos dominated Egypt for about two hundred years and were followed by the Persians, Romans, Greeks, and Assyrians, each of whom caucasianized Egypt.

The European transatlantic enslavement of Africans was started by the Portuguese in the fourteenth century. Ki-Zerbo (1981) has suggested that before chattel slavery, Africa and Europe were at the same level of development in terms of science and technology. By any standard of measurement including appreciation for the social function of science, sociopolitical organization, community cohesion, housing, religious consistency, and the creative arts, African civilizations surpassed that of Europe up until the fifteenth century (Du Bois, 1976). Du Bois asserts that the enslavement trade retarded Africa's development.

It is estimated that about one hundred million people were removed from Africa as a consequence of the trade. This grossly immoral capture and sale of humans promoted the disintegration of African civilization and caused the destruction of human possibilities. The European enslavers' vicious activities left many areas in Africa permanently depopulated. Moreover, raiding to enslave Africans was of such a violent nature that many areas were preoccupied with the maintenance of personal security to the detriment of socioeconomic development (Rodney, 1972).

Another negative consequence of the transatlantic trade was that in exchange for those Africans who were to be enslaved, Europeans flooded Africa with cheap and flawed commercial products. Africans' preference for Western goods adversely impacted their production of indigenous goods including cotton goods and metal. While the enslavement trade contributed to the underdevelopment of Africa, European countries such as Germany, Portugal, Italy, Britain, Spain, France, and the United States accumulated massive amounts of capital which was key in their transition from mercantile to industrial capitalism (Rodney, 1972; Williams, 1980).

"Cheap European goods pushed in and threw the native products out of competition. Rum and gin displaced the milder native drinks. The beautiful patterned cloth, brocades, and velvets disappeared before their cheap imitations in Manchester calicos. Methods of work were lost and forgotten" (Du Bois, 1965, p. 78).

Furthermore, the trade in Africans undermined African solidarity. Africans were forced to flee to safer havens in the hinterland and to areas of difficult access in order to escape European enslavers and their African cohorts (Kodjo, 1987; Williams, 1976). This is one reason for the great mixture of ethnic groups and languages in contemporary Africa and led to the development of disunity and mutual suspicion as a way of life for African people. Colonial boundaries drawn by Europeans in 1884-1885 compounded this disunity.

The enslavement and colonization of Africans also fostered a false sense of White superiority and class privilege; the mindset of Africans became informed by feelings of racial inferiority, while Whites came to internalize the myth of their racial superiority.

Since the enslavement period, a psychology of dependency has blocked the creative genius and productive efficacy of Africans. In addition Africa's best producers—her most energetic, intelligent, and sturdy African sons and daughters have been systematically destroyed by Europeans for more than three centuries. It will be demonstrated more fully in the next chapter that the systematic dehumanization of people of African descent has only undergone superficial changes in more recent times.

Effects of Colonialism

Africans lost power and control over their internal affairs under colonialism. The colonization of Africa liquidated preexisting states and destroyed the moral foundations of established societies. Colonial rule destroyed the right and ability of Africans to chart their development and remain the authors of their own destiny. Under colonialism, Europeans appropriated the social institutions of Africa and attempted to abrogate African cultural traditions and ideals to ensure the successful imposition of European cultural standards (Rodney, 1972). For instance, Du Bois (1975) emphasized that "by the end of the nineteenth century the degradation of Africa was as complete as organized

The Marginalization of the African World

human means could make it. Chieftains, representing a thousand years of striving human culture, were decked out in second hand London top-hats, while Europe snickered" (p. 78).

In general, notwithstanding the arguments on the colonialists' positive contributions to Africa, the testimony of history is that Europeans brought the worst that civilization could offer to Africa (Davidson, 1974). The oppressed of African descent must also recognize that although colonialism lasted in most parts of Africa for about seventy years, it was nevertheless a major historical source for the marginalization of the African world to the present day.

Before colonization African economies were relatively self-sufficient and closed to foreign control, while economic links between Africa and the rest of the world were progressing. During the precolonial period Africa did not have to rely on food aid from the international community.

Colonial production relations in Africa destroyed or transformed the majority of self-sufficient African economies (Adu Boahen, 1990). The colonialists, by insisting that all processing of locally produced raw materials and agricultural products occur outside of the colonies, prevented African industrialization. In discussing the political economy of colonialism, Adu Boahen (1987) asserted that "Africans were encouraged to produce what they did not consume and to consume what they did not produce, a clear proof of the exploitative nature of the colonial political economy. It is lamentable that this legacy has not changed materially in most African countries. To this day they have to rely on the importation of rice, maize, edible oil, flour and other food stuffs to survive" (p. 102). He also pointed out that under colonialism, both intra-African and inter-African economic links were broken. Equally significant is the observation that the arbitrary and artificial boundaries drawn by Europeans set up restrictive parameters of economic activities; Africans became consumers of manufactured goods and producers of raw materials for export. The economies of African nation-states are still externally oriented towards Europe.

Another contributing variable to Africa's underdevelopment was military violence. Each colonial power that allotted itself a portion of African territory conducted military operations in its pacification campaigns. For example, the German General Von Trotha saw to the slaying of three quarters of the Herroros, the main ethnic group of Namibia (Stoecker, 1986). The violence of colonialism which included mass executions, forced labor, excessive taxation, and ruthless punishments forced Africans to flee across international boundaries or withdraw into the inaccessible parts of the colony where refugee settlements were formed.

It is clear that one of the most detrimental consequences of the colonial period—the partitioning of Africa—was balkanization which occurred in the 1880s and continues to effectively undermine the unity of the continent. In order to conquer and rule Africans, it was necessary for Europeans to concretize divisions and foster conflicts among Blacks. To accomplish these objectives the European colonialists deliberately divided cultural groups inside new colonial boundaries and combined different, unrelated ethnic groups to effectively pit Blacks against each other. This has led to internal ethno-religious and regional strife which have served chiefly to destroy African lives and mire Africa into grinding poverty. In short, Africans have surrendered to tribalism. As Hadjor (1987) reminds us: "it is a colonial creation which now haunts the African way of life" (p. 63) and makes nation-building especially problematic. One suggestion is that postcolonial tribalism flourished because once the declaration of national sovereignties became fixed, this reinforced rivalries over scare resources. For Davidson (1992), "this divisive rivalry was then discovered to be tribalism: that is, the reinforcement of kinship or other local-scale alliances competing against other such alliances" (p. 185). He further suggested that tribalism flourished because "the separatist nation-states gave full reign to elitist rivalries" (p. 186).

Africa's current fragmentation and preoccupation with national sovereignties have resulted in border disputes which threaten continental solidarity and the formation of a united and prosperous Africa. Thom (1986) predicts that the widening gap between militarily weak and strong nations, coupled with the assertion of national interests, will increase the scope, duration, and destructiveness of future conflicts between African states. According to Thom, the ability of the Organization of African Unity (OAU) to use its influence to preserve the existing boundaries will weaken greatly in the near future. He further predicts that interstate contests will be among the most significant wars in Africa. Moreover, there is no solid inter-African coordination to even balance the growing boldness of several African countries (Ostheimer, 1986).

It is quite distressing that most postcolonial African leaders have consistently disregarded the rallying appeal for Pan-Africanism. It is also critical to emphasize that colonial rule is implicated in the ruling elite's refusal to make the psychological choice to build a union of African states. The reader must bear in mind that during the colonial period, Africa's ruling elite were properly indoctrinated with European values. Entry into the new elite was gained by those Blacks who were able to enjoy commercial success under colonial rule. In sum, Africa's ruling elite have steadfastly sought for the satisfaction of their own personal and selfish needs for esteem, power, wealth, and privilege. Their minds have been hardened against the advice of great African leaders on how to create the union of African states. According to Nyerere (1968), this would require the transfer of some of the sovereignty of these states from their national units to a single unit, and, among other things, "coordinate and facilitate the economic development of Africa as a whole, in such a manner as to ensure the well-being of every part of the continent, conserving the many-colored fabric of African civilization, while greatly strengthening and enlarging it" (Davidson, 1969, p. 317).

Disregarding the rallying cry for Pan-Africanism, the Black ruling elite has permitted Africa's dependency on the West as a means of ensuring their own power, wealth, and prosperity. As a result, the continent lacks effective unity in economic, political, and military affairs. Africa is thereby unable to defend itself against the racial hostilities of Europeans. For instance, with the assistance of the West, the Republic of South Africa gained the distinction of being the only country south of the Sahara that had the capability of supplying its own equipment and weapons needs. Consequently, the White South African government was able to act with impunity against Black nations who ever unable to effectively retaliate against the aggression of this racist government. Clearly intra-African cooperation was (and is) the only hope for the effective protection of African interests and national security. However, several African governments instead opted to defend their own selfishly defined interests by forging economic ties with the racist South African regime (Morna, 1991).

Colonization has left other lasting imprints on people of African descent. Colonialism taught Africans that for their development they had to forget their cultural past, divorce themselves from Africa's foundations, and embrace European models (Davidson, 1992). Virtually all of independent Africa relies on European models of society for defining their political structures and objectives. The europeanization of Africa can be seen in the continent's academic institutions, its print and broadcast media, military, and other aspects of African life that have been conditioned to mimic European values and lifestyle. Chinweizu (1987) posits that Africa continues to turn to the outside world to receive its concepts, food, economic and military assistance, religions, and languages. So, without its own indigenous institutions, Africa has lost the ability to control its affairs (Hadjor, 1987).

Africans have continued to serve in the oppressors' armies for the protection of the oppressors' interests, while the substantial rewards for which these deafricanized persons fought fail to materialize. During the colonial period of conquest "most of the armies of European imperialists consisted of African soldiers and thousands of African auxiliaries usually recruited from annexed or allied territories, and it was only the officer corps that was usually European" (Adu Boahen, 1987, p. 56). The Portuguese military system depended upon "large forces of African auxiliaries called the guerra pretia (black war), raised from loyal chiefs; hired as mercenaries, or press-ganged into service. Between 1575 and 1925, some 5,000 to 20,000 of these indigenous troops were used to support the 2,000 or less Europeans of the first-line colonial army in Angola" (Gibson, 1972, p. 204). During the Mozambicans' struggles against the Portuguese (1920-1968), Black soldiers of the Portuguese army outnumbered Frelimo liberation forces by three to one (Seegers, 1986).

Furthermore, many "Black-ruled" states are totally dependent on Western and Eastern countries for military training and supplies. Black Africa's weaponry is more often than not refurbished Korean war and Vietnam era equipment (Snyder, 1986). People of African descent have failed to transform European military doctrines and methods to meet their own indigenous military needs. African armies still cling to a colonial mentality which states that the ideal soldier should be "illiterate, uncontaminated by mission education, from a remote area, physically tough and politically unsophisticated" (Snyder, 1986, p. 114). Africans have also failed to develop indigenous defense industries, forcing them to remain technological hostages of external powers (Snyder, 1986).

Another disturbing observation is that, due to the socioeconomic and political atrophy experienced by most African societies, there are those Africans who have openly expressed their nostalgia for the caretakership of the former European colonialists. At the other extreme, there are majority Black societies such as Bermuda, the Cayman Islands, the islands of the Netherlands Antilles, Martinique, Guadeloupe, French Guiana, the British Virgin Islands, and Anguilla that steadfastly refuse to become fully independent of the former European colonial powers. In fact the only remaining pressure for independence comes from colonial administrators in London and The Hague who are eager to trim expenses (French, 1991).

It is equally appalling that the ruling elite of supposedly "independent" African nations, both on the Continent and in the diaspora, continue to surrender these countries to the exploitation of European imperialists. A colonial mentality has motivated these Blacks to rely on the oppressors to gratify their basic needs and manage the affairs of their national life. Obviously the collective consciousness of these Blacks has failed to develop to a more mature psychological and political level and this then suggests that such dependency on the oppressors, depicts the lingering doubts on the part of the oppressed about making it in the world on their own.

Even postcolonial African nations that strive for full independence have seen their efforts thwarted by Europeans. For example in the 1990s the approximately ninety thousand Whites who live among a population of nearly ten million in independent Zimbabwe still yield considerable influence over the country's economy and commercial farming sector. They cling to a deep-seated sense of racial superiority, insist on segregating themselves from Black Zimbabweans, and are in the country only to extract economic wealth in the same way that their ancestors came to prospect for gold (Meldrum, 1991). President Mugabe's government was forced to initiate bold measures to acquire portions of land held by White farmers (Perlez, 1992).

Similarly, after nearly twenty years of armed Black liberation struggle, Namibia gained independence from South Africa in 1990. After independence Sam Nujoma's government, the South West Africa People's Organization (Swapo), embarked on a national policy of racial reconciliation. Predictably White Namibians displayed their contempt for this policy by daily abusing and exploiting Blacks. Most of these eighty-two thousand Whites occupy the top slots of the economy, live in luxury, and segregate themselves from Blacks. While approximately four thousand White farmers owned the bulk of the arable land, 90 percent of the 1.3 million Black Namibians were land poor and poverty stricken. In 1992, the Swapo party announced the launching of a bloodless "second liberation struggle" to end these racial inequities and equally redistribute the land (Kelso, 1992).

The Marginalization of the African World 77

The enslavement period and subsequent colonial domination disorganized the African world to its very core. These historical events have negatively impacted the cultural, political, psychological, military, economic, social, and spiritual existence of people of African descent. Any interest in the African world must be informed by a careful study of the enslavement and colonization of Africans. The thrust of the subsequent discussion is to further identify some of the debilitating effects of these internal factors.

Debilitating Internal Factors

While acknowledging the valiant antienslavement and anticolonial struggles of people of African descent, this author concurs with those who argue that people of African descent must examine those structural, cultural, and individual factors that have allowed us to become key participants in our own oppression. According to Kodjo (1987), during the early period of Africa's history, African societies were organized into social castes which, through appointed representatives, were associated with the government. Kodjo contends that African societies were under the control of high priests and that the masses had little access to the knowledge which could help them control their natural environment. Once the castes of the high priests died out, African societies were deprived of scientific and technological memory. Furthermore, Africa's decline was compounded by problems of local governments, specifically the ambitions of provincial governors who were eager to break away from central authority. According to Ajayi (1965), some of the earliest African empires failed to create a satisfactory system of succession to replace kings and other rulers. The political vacuum fostered rivalries and disputes in which the strongest individual emerged as the ruler. These internal revolts weakened African kingdoms such as fourteenth century Mali.

Europeans took advantage of the internal disintegration of traditional African societies. Although prior to the devastating enslavement trade many African states were as well organized, if not more so, than some European states, by the nineteenth century, Europe had perfected its technology and was to emerge militarily superior to Africa.

Many Africans, out of sheer greed and in an attempt to exact revenge against previous allies and enemies, sold their people to slave traders. Several African societies, including the people of Dahomey, the Swahili-speaking groups on the East coast of Africa, and the people of the Niger delta on the Guinea coast, accepted partnership in the enslavement trade. In return these societies received consumer goods, firearms, and gunpowder. However, as Davidson (1991) pointed out, they paid a high price in social and political disruptions and production loss. As he noted African societies which profited from the trade remained for the most part within their traditional limits of production and organization. On the other hand the labor and profits yielded by the enslavement of Africans helped build the capital accumulation for the English and French industrial revolutions and laid the foundation for modern American civilization.

In summary, internal and external factors precipitated the decline of Africa and allowed for the perennial difficulties faced by people of African descent. One can also observe in contemporary Africans some of our long-standing psychological responses to European domination. For instance, the infamous legacy of those ancestors who sought mainly to ensure their own personal security during the enslavement and colonial epochs continues. Naturally, such preoccupations have been shown to detract from the African's full involvement in meaningful human praxis to advance the interests of the African world.

The Contemporary Conditions of People of African Descent

Given the historical background described above, some of the specific issues facing Africans on the continent and in the diaspora can be identified. Some estimates suggest that Africa has about 400-500 million people, approximately 250 million of whom are poor by anybody's standards (Barnet, 1990). Of the continents in the world, Africa is the only one in which, if present trends continue, the majority of her people living in poverty will increase by the year 2000 (Britain, 1992). Universally agreed upon indicators of a status of countries. Among these are access to clean drinking water, adult literacy, daily calorie intake, health care, infant mortality, life expectancy, income, gross national output, and military preparedness. Africa compares unfavorably with Europe and other continents on these and other indicators.

Africa has been identified as the continent with extreme human suffering and with the worst living conditions in the world. Living conditions are dismal in Mozambique, Angola, Chad, Mali, Ghana, Somalia, Niger, Burkina Faso, Zaire, Benin, and Malawi. It is essential to point out that countries south of the Sahara (Black Africa), which were double victim of Western style enslavement and colonization, are among the poorest in the region and indeed in the world at large. For example, the annual per capita income in some countries of sub-Saharan Africa is below $200.00.

The Food Crisis

Agriculture has historically been the mainstay of Africa's economy. However Africa, once an agrarian continent, has lost the ability to feed itself. Millions of Africans have starved to death and millions more risk starvation. Some projections are that hunger or death threaten a third of the 100 million people inhabiting affected areas of Southern and Eastern Africa.

In Angola there was such a desperate demand for food that armed bandits reportedly raided public transportation and attacked people (Noble, 1990). Once Angola was the world's fourth largest producer of coffee and the fifth largest of diamonds, now, many basic food items must be imported. The Angolan government's sixteen years of civil war with Jonas

Savimbi's National Union for the Total Independence of Angola (UNITA) rebel movement has devastated this nation. The United Nations estimated that basic installations and services suffered more than $30 billion in material damage from 1980-1992. Despite the signing of a historic peace accord in 1991, Angola's drought has provided an impetus for impoverished soldiers to damage the peace accord with opportunistic violence to obtain food. The reader should bear in mind that beginning in the 1960s the Angolan masses experienced a fourteen-year armed liberation struggle against the Portuguese colonialists. On the eve of independence in November 1975 the nationalist parties turned their guns against each other in a pathological quest for power and control. The physical, material, and psychological miseries of war-fatigued and starving Angolan masses were extremely severe in the early 1990s.

Likewise, the sixteen-year civil war between the rebel Mozambique National Resistance (Renamo) movement and the Mozambican government resulted in one quarter of Mozambique's fifteen million people dependent on food aid for their survival, while over 70 percent are living in absolute poverty. This civil war has taken more than one million lives and caused more than 1.5 million people to seek refuge in neighboring countries. An estimated 800,000 Mozambican refugees are living in neighboring Malawi and are dependent on international food relief while about four million Mozambicans are refugees in their own country (Meldrum, 1991). Mozambique has been so devastated by this civil war that 76 percent of its gross national income consists of foreign assistance which exceeds the average 11 percent for all other sub-Saharan African states (Ayisi, 1991). These inter-African conflicts have been sustained by massive outside assistance from the long-standing enemies of people of African descent including the South African government.

Black Africa's fragile economies are incapable of alleviating food shortages as well as the other negative consequences of drought. These severe droughts also aggravate other related problems such as balance of payments, debt repayment, food imports, and urbanization. Millions of starving Africans have fled the rural areas for the towns and cities placing more severe strains on the urban areas already weak economy.

The problems of the African world are further complicated by the fact that a recurrent theme is the forced removal of Africans from their proximal social environments. An estimated fifteen million or more Africans are displaced from their homes due to conflict and armed violence, while others are forced to leave their homes in search of food. Africa's current drought and food shortages have aggravated the problems of these refugees who dwell in squalid squatter camps both within and without their social environmental boundaries. Refugees are usually deprived of proper nutrition, health, social, educational, and other basic human needs. Due to competition for scarce resources, these refugees are often hostile to one another and vulnerable to attacks from their hosts (Prendergast, 1991). There are several devastating psychological and sociocultural consequences for those uprooted from their homes. Refugees are not easily assimilated into the host communities and as a result they experience feelings of alienation and despair which often lead to social and psychological starvation and physical death (Bulhan, 1987; Schultheis, 1989). It has been suggested that continental defense forces could safeguard these refugees until regional conflicts are resolved or other solutions could be worked out between central and/or host governments and refugees (Ostheimer, 1986).

Food self-sufficiency has receded due to the colonialists' plunder of Africa's soil, civil wars, drought, poor physical infrastructures, inadequate supply of drought-resistant seeds, overgrazing, the absence of deep wells and catchment dams, rapid urbanization, inappropriate public policies and management strategies, and desertification. It is estimated that Africa is losing forests at the rate of 1.3 million hectares a year (Timberlake, 1985). Despite being reduced by some of the aforementioned sources, Africa's water resources have the potential to irrigate the arid areas. Yet, African leaders have largely failed to exercise the political will to engineer the development of human and technical resources to harness the water supplies and meet the needs of the masses.

On the other hand, despite Africa's agricultural crises, whatever agricultural production does occur is geared toward international and urban demands and tastes (Abubaker, 1989). For example, a disproportionate amount of Africa's food imports of wheat and rice are for the urban population. And, up to the middle of the 1980s, twenty-five years after independence, Africa's agriculture produced more for the satisfaction of consumer markets abroad rather than for the feeding of African populations.

As can be gleaned from the discussion, external factors including declines in foreign aid and foreign investment, worsening terms of trade, declining exports, both in price and quantities, as well as increasing imports in both price and volume are also involved in Africa's food crisis (Sparks, 1990). Africa is incapable of absorbing the external shocks imposed by these Western economic decisions. To illustrate, Africa's compensation for falling prices has been to exploit much of its arable land for the production of cash crops for export. Meanwhile there is a paucity of funds for agricultural and technological development. Profound poverty and human suffering are the predictable and debilitating outcomes.

It is equally important to underscore the argument that Western economic policies and strategies are for the West's maintenance of the world's wealth and resources. Independent African countries must seek to disengage themselves from the Western economic system. The African world must continue to forge greater intraracial cooperation and develop economic structures that are controlled by Africans primarily for the benefits of Africans. Africa must invest in rural agricultural development to first meet its domestic need. Once Africa attains a level of productivity to generate a surplus, then those funds should be directed toward research, training, and technology for African progress and development (Abubakar, 1989).

The Health Crisis

Many Africans die from preventable illnesses caused by the general disintegration of public services and the poverty of national economies. For instance, cholera has been sweeping through several African countries causing excess death rates that range from 6-10 percent of the population in some African countries and are as high as 30 percent in certain areas (Altman, 1991). Cholera epidemics are primarily caused by improper disposal of human waste that contaminates drinking water and food with cholera bacteria. It has been estimated that approximately 80 percent of all illness in Africa's less developed communities can be associated with inadequate water supplies or poor sanitation (Sparks, 1990). Safe water is out of reach for 63 percent of Africans (Africa Report, 1990).

In general, Europeans are expected to live into their mid-seventies while the life expectancy of a West African is forty-seven years and in the rural areas it is estimated at thirty-five years. Northern Africans average fifty-eight years and Africans living in Middle Africa have a life expectancy of forty-nine years. Africans living in the Southern African regions of Botswana and Lesotho have a life expectancy in the early fifties, in Ethiopia and Sierra Leone life expectancy is at forty-two years and in Guinea-Bissau the average life expectancy is thirty-nine years.

The brevity of African lives can also be observed in the Western Hemisphere. For Haitians it is fifty-four years, and for Black men in Harlem the rate of survival beyond the age of forty is lower than in Bangladesh—one of the lowest income countries in the world. A recent study indicated that White racism, vicious poverty, inadequate housing, psychological stress, substance abuse, and inadequate access to health care are all causative agents in the excessive deaths of these Blacks (McCord and Freeman, 1990).

AIDS is a leading cause of fatalities both in continental and diasporan Africans. Some forecasts have estimated seven million AIDS-related deaths in Africa during the 1990s. In the United

States, AIDS was the tenth leading cause of deaths for Blacks, while ranking fifteenth for the overall American population. The critical point to bear in mind is that AIDS is killing our people during their most productive years, particularly between the ages of twenty and forty years of age. Both Africa's educated elite and villagers have suffered excess AIDS-related deaths and the medical establishment is projecting further surges in the AIDS epidemic in Africa and other non-White communities.

Concerning infant mortality, more than one hundred African babies per one thousand live births die before the first year of life on the African continent. The figure is closer to two hundred in some countries such as Mali. In Angola, 1988 figures indicate that twenty-nine of every one hundred children died before their fifth year of life. Sub-Saharan Africa has one of the highest infant mortality rates in the world. According to a United Nations report, Africa's share of global child and infant deaths is expected to increase to 40 percent in the next decade—up from 30 percent just five years ago. The figures in the United States are just as disturbing, 17.9 African-American infants die per one thousand, compared to 8.6 for White infants.

Inadequate medical services are responsible for the deaths of African children at disproportionate rates from preventable illnesses such as malaria, abscesses, tetanus, and infections. AIDS is also causing massive fatalities among Black children. For instance, some estimates suggest that the devastating fatalities from AIDS have created ten million orphans on the continent, one-third of whom are also infected with the AIDS virus.

Africa has more rural populations than any other continent in the world. Yet, most of the health care is concentrated in the urban areas of Africa, leaving the majority of the population without adequate public health facilities. At the same time, the continent is reported to annually spend only $2.00 per capita on health care. Many Africans, particularly the inhabitants of rural areas, remain uninformed about the behavioral changes necessary to combat the spread of HIV infections. Moreover, African leaders have not persuaded themselves to display their political

commitment in the fight against AIDS.
It should also be observed that this gap between urban and rural areas was widened by European colonialists who concentrated all modern infrastructures such as hospitals, schools, telecommunication networks, and employment opportunities and so forth in urban areas. This was done for the efficient administration of their colonies and to maximize European exploitation of Africa. With regard to education, Rodney (1972) wrote that the "unevenness in educational levels reflected the unevenness of economic exploitation and different rates at which the different parts of a colony entered the money economy" (p. 243).

Crises in Industry and Technology

Western Europe receives 65 percent of Africa's mineral and energy exports, Japan 15 percent, North America 4 percent. Africa plays no significant role as a producer of manufactured goods, contributing an estimated .5 percent to world production (Kodjo, 1987). The entire continent accounted for about 3 percent of world trade and (Barnet, 1990) in 1992 represented only 1 percent of world trade (Britain, 1992).

Africa is a market for the manufactured goods of industrial powers. Now that stringent regulations and costly safety laws in Europe and the United States have pushed toxic waste disposal costs up to $2,500 a ton, waste brokers have turned to Africa. Several African nations signed contracts, out of greed and in other instances sheer ignorance, to bury nuclear and industrial waste. Many continental Africans complain that the Western toxic merchants did not inform them about the contents of the lethal imports. United States companies, for instance, relied instead on vague and misleading phrases such as "pure dry cleaning solvent," "complex organic matter," and "ordinary industrial wastes" in describing lethal cargos. In addition, Europeans reportedly buried waste near fish and water supplies and even in populated communities (Third World Network,

1989). Even as Somalia's population and natural resources were being destroyed by the combined effects of war and drought, there were reports of Italian firms' plans to ship toxic waste there which would further destroy this country's ecosystem and compromise the health status of its people. Similar to Mussolini's Italian forces who used poison gas in the mid-1930s to advance Italian imperialism in the Horn of Africa, Italian toxic merchants intend to profit from Somalia's vulnerabilities and tragedies. As one writer stated in the Nigerian African Concord newspaper "that Italy did not contemplate Australia or South Africa or some other place for industrial waste re-echoes what Europe has always thought of Africa: A wasteland. And the people who live there waste people" (Brooke, 1989). Indeed, the World Bank officials stated that poor countries should become the repositories of these deadly substances (Shepherd, 1992).

Diasporan Black communities are also victims of environmental racism. Bellegarde-Smith (1990) informed us that "in January 1988, the Khiang-Sea had dumped 4,000 tons of toxic waste from Philadelphia near Gonaives, Haiti's fourth-largest city and the site of Haiti's independence in 1804, and this event became a symbol of the contempt in which Haiti has traditionally been held. It reminded Haitians that in June 1872, two German frigates in an exercise of gunboat diplomacy had seized two Haitian warships. Upon leaving after their demands had been satisfied, the Germans had defecated on the Haitian flag on both ships before abandoning them" (p. 177-178).

In the United States, a disproportionate number of African-Americans experience health problems and death from industrial pollution and toxic contamination. Pollution-related asthma is killing our people five times the rate it kills Whites (Kennedy & Rivera, 1992). Black communities are the primary sites for the establishment of waste treatment plants, chemical dumps, and toxic waste incinerators by industrial corporations and the United States government (Schneider, 1991). Three of the five largest hazardous waste landfills are located in majority Black and Hispanic neighborhoods and account for 40 percent of

America's total estimated landfill capacity. The nation's largest toxic waste dump is in Emelle, Alabama, a poverty-stricken city which is 80 percent Black. More than 50 percent of Black and Hispanic people live in communities with hazardous waste dumps and "three of every four toxic-waste dumps that fail to comply with the (Environmental Protection Agency's) regulations are in Black and Hispanic neighborhoods" (Kennedy & Rivera, 1992, A19).

The Debt Crisis

There is no remedy in sight for another trauma, namely the continent's escalating debt. This stood at 150 billion U.S. dollars in 1985 and had increased to over 272 billion dollars by 1990. sub-Saharan Africa's debt rate reached $174 billion in 1990. Debt servicing takes 30 percent of export earnings, but as Britain (1992) wrote, "this is only two-thirds of the debt, as the impossibility of full interest payment is widely recognized" (p. 46). The World Bank's structural adjustment programs have contributed to starvation and poverty throughout the region.

The Western creditors structural adjustment policies for Africa's debt have called for reductions in per capita consumption and imports. This has been accompanied by disastrous human and social consequences. In attempting to meet their loan obligations, African countries have responded with reductions in food subsidies, devaluation of their currency, and by spending less money on education, health services, and other infrastructures, further damaging the growth of countries in the region. In the 1980s, drastic reductions in expenditures on health, education, and other social programs were accompanied with increased hunger, infant mortalities, deteriorations in nutritional levels, unemployment, and lower incomes (Africa Report, 1990).

The World Bank has suggested that the debt problem is due to a lack of financial discipline and poor management in many African countries. Turok (1989) has argued that the real cause is the collapse of African commodity prices at the international level down to 1950 levels and the deterioration of the terms of trade for African nations. However, one cannot overlook the fact that Africa's leaders and the elite have enriched themselves by amassing personal fortunes from international aid and channeling these funds outside of the continent. Such activities have been detrimental to Africa's growth and development.

Diasporan Black nations are also in deep economic crises due to their foreign debts. In Jamaica, the national external debt in 1991 was $3.8 billion. To meet its loan obligations, Jamaica instituted higher taxation and drastic cuts in public sector employment. These economic adjustments resulted in increases in the unemployment and crime rates, increases in the cost of consumer and food items, and increases in reported cases of malnutrition. Structural adjustment policies have also resulted in deep cuts in the Jamaican government's expenditures on public health, education, low cost housing, and public transportation. As Levitt (1991) advised, "Jamaica must free itself of the mentality of dependence, including dependence on aid. The modalities of the IMF/World Bank designed adjustment programs breed a psychology of failure and impotence. As one of Jamaica's more dynamic politicians put it, 'many of us have entrapped our minds in the chains of inferiority and defeatist thinking. The IMF cannot free our minds. All the foreign aid in the world cannot free our minds. We have to do it ourselves and until we come out of self-defeating mental chains, we have no hope of surviving our problems'" (p. 63).

There is absolutely no altruism and empathy associated with aid from the West. For example, although Africans are responsible for payment, Western creditors oftentimes insist that projects be instituted by Western companies. In addition, aid agencies are likely to refuse funding the development of public enterprises that would cut the flow of raw materials and strategic resources to the industrialized countries. Aid and technical assistance from the West are to the advantage of the donor countries and represent colonization without responsibility. Africa's debt permits the West to interfere in her national affairs and falsifies claims of self-reliance and self-determination. Another thesis is that the World Bank and the International Monetary Fund represent the harsh face of Western capitalist interests whose objective seems to be to block the development in the Third World by the easiest mechanisms, that is, by the imposition of debt payment. This is said to be a new war without guns (Turok, 1989).

The relentless racist assaults against people of African descent are largely due to the fact that the African world is burdened by pervasive poverty, underdevelopment, and dependency on the West. Although there have been instances of successful victories against White supremacy, for the most part, Black Africa's debilitating social, economic, military, and political crises has disabled her from posing serious threats to global White supremacy. The marginality of the African world has served to reinforce negative racist stereotypes about the inferiority of people of African descent and the natural superiority of Whites. For over three thousand years, White supremacists have acted with impunity against people of African descent.

The African world has the task of regaining its sovereignty and independence. Africa's political rulers must demonstrate authentic loyalty to the African masses. Our victory over White domination will be assured only when people of African descent make the psychological choice to become authentic strugglers. This ideal struggler is convinced that we, the people of African descent, must be the real determiners of our destiny. Authentic strugglers accept personal responsibility for the upliftment and advancement of the African world.

The following chapter attempts to examine the anti-African attitudes and practices which are especially palpable and virulent in the Western world. I fully recognize that anti-African practices can be found on the continent, however time and space do not allow for an examination of these issues in South Africa and other African countries. I have instead decided to restrict my focus to anti-African practices in the diaspora. My main aim is for the oppressed of African descent to understand why it is critical for them to wipe from their eyes all delusions of freedom and human dignity and allow for their psychological lives to be informed by an African collective liberation consciousness.

Chapter IV

ANTI-AFRICAN PRACTICES AND DIASPORAN AFRICANS

> We need some African power, some great center of the race where our physical, pecuniary, and intellectual strength may be collected. We need some spot whence such an influence may go forth in behalf of the race as shall be felt by the nations. We are now so scattered and divided we can do nothing...So long as we live simply by the sufferance of the nations, we must expect to be subject to their caprices.
>
> Edward Wilmot Blyden

There are over three hundred million Africans living outside of the boundaries of Africa. Black skin color has been a stimulus for White tyranny in the West. White interest has been served by limiting the quality and extent of Africans' participation in important life activities related to wealth, power, and privilege.

Much has been written on this topic for countries such as the United States, Britain, and Brazil. In contrast, there appears to be a paucity of literature on several European countries, Asia, and the Caribbean region. What follows are general descriptions of the subordination of black-skinned people throughout the diaspora. Interspersed are historical and contemporary explanations for the anti-African practices of the countries discussed.

Anti-African Activities in Europe

There have been increasing reports of Europeans' instinctive racial hatred being satisfied through anti-African practices (Kinzer, 1991; Ibrahim, 1990; Riding, 1990). The media has reported on the racially inspired murders of Africans by White supremacists in Europe. Africans living in Europe have reported on the pain of discrimination and abuse (Simmons, 1990). The evidence is overwhelming that institutionalized racism has encouraged and supported racist assaults against Africans in France, Germany, Netherlands, Italy, Norway, Sweden, Switzerland, Austria, Spain, Britain, and other European countries (Evrigenis, 1985). A European tendency, one which is shared by Blacks, is to attribute these anti-African practices to the social pressures of unemployment, poverty, and the shortage of housing. These social problems are purported to be caused by the massive influx of foreigners from Third World countries. However, many of these shocking racist attacks are occurring in regions of Europe where there are said to be no patterns of dislocation and poverty. Moreover, according to the authorities, the perpetrators of such racist crimes usually have jobs and housing (Kinzer, 1991).

Germany

Blacks began migrating to Germany from German colonies during the nineteenth century. Evidence shows that from the colonial period to the present day the Black presence has been despised by Germans (Opitz, Oguntoye and Schultz, 1992).

Consistent with most European countries, Germans are convinced that only Whites belong in their country. An immigration law ("Auslandergesetz") of the Federal Republic of Germany became valid on January 1, 1991 and places severe restrictions on the migration of non-Whites to Germany.

Blacks born in Germany are viewed as unwanted foreigners and therefore undeserving of the rights and privileges of German society. Black-skinned people are considered inferior and culturally backward to White Germans. Black youth are persistently denied access to advanced studies and are relegated to nonacademic and service occupations. Employment and housing discrimination is pervasive. The recent unification of the two German states has been accompanied with increased racial violence towards non-Whites.

As a result of these anti-African practices, according to Opitz, Oguntoye, and Schultz (1992), "Afro-Germans" have internalized the myth of their racial inferiority and possess low racial self-esteem. In the presence of Whites many Blacks either avoid drawing attention to their Africanness or make desperate attempts to be White. Others act in racially stereotypic ways by being funny and affable to add flavor to the lives of White people.

The German government recently stated that xenophobia is a totally unacceptable disgrace to Germany and therefore violence against foreigners will be confronted with the utmost legal firmness and strictness (Protzman, 1992). However, if the past is any indication, German judges will continue to sanction racist assaults on people of African descent by failing to punish the White perpetrators (Kinzer, 1992).

The ideals of communism—equalitarianism and international idealism—may have inhibited the more overt expression of primal predatory and materialistic responses of Europeans to black-skinned people. These inhibitions have been lifted by the collapse of the socialist system in Eastern Europe. The eventual unification of Europe simply means that the White world will be an even stronger and hostile political, military, and economic force against people of African descent.

I must emphasize that the oppressed of African descent ought not to neglect the fundamental premise that the intent of various European nations is to remain fiercely White and view the intrusion of non-Whites as a threat to their right to preserve their own culture, language, and religious traditions. Other poverty-stricken areas of the world have taken in refugees without the rampant xenophobic hatred shown by the Germans. Moreover, political organizations with blatant xenophobic and White nationalist platforms have mushroomed throughout Europe. These flagrantly racist organizations are now enjoying political success in states such as the Netherlands, France, Germany, and Britain. Also, several European nations have recently instituted immigration policies to restrict the number of non-White foreign residents.

In responding to a reporter's comments on the recent racial atrocities against non-Whites in Germany, one German citizen was reported to have replied, "Let them stay in the bush...This is Germany. They don't belong here. German women with Black babies can you believe that" (Kinzer, 1991, p. A8).

Britain

Following the second major European war of this century, West Indians of African descent began a major migration to Britain and somehow expected to be treated as equal citizens by their former colonial rulers. A colonial education had instilled in these Black settlers reverence for the 'mother country'; they considered themselves part of the British empire (Fryer, 1984). On arrival these immigrants were relegated to low paying jobs and materially and socially disadvantaged neighborhoods (Lashley, 1986).

The unrealistic expectations of the Black immigrants reflect the attitude of the oppressed to ignore the testimony of history on the racist nature of their oppressors. In the mid 1700s, with an increase in the number of enslaved Blacks, White Britons began to press for legislation to preserve racial purity by expelling Blacks from Britain and restricting their future entry. Since then Britain has continued to pass antiimmigration laws. Laws passed in 1962 and 1971 limited the flow of non-White groups to people who had been given work permits. Further rules were proposed in 1991 to reduce the number of immigrants of color, particularly Africans, from settling in Great Britain (Schmidt, 1991).

In 1965, while enacting racially restrictive immigration policies, Britain introduced its first law aimed at fighting racial discrimination. The British government, however, has never provided the human and financial resources to effect changes in the racial status quo (Lashley, 1986).

Scotland Yard's latest statistics showed 3,373 incidents of racial assault or harassment in London in 1991, an increase of 16 percent over the 1990 figures. About fifty of these cases involved physical assault (Schmidt, 1992). These must be considered conservative estimates because many racial assaults are not reported by non-Whites to the 98 percent White police force. Racism by the British police is manifested in the police murders of Black people, the arbitrary arrest of Black people, the refusal to provide Black people with protection against racial violence, the unwillingness to persecute White attackers, the use of unnecessary brute force in arresting Blacks, and the wanton harassment of Black women, men, and youth. As is the case in other countries regulated by White supremacy, Blacks in Britain are likely to receive harsher treatment than Whites in the criminal justice sys-

Anti-African Practices and Diasporan Africans 97

tem. While Black people make up 4.7 percent of the population in Britain and Wales, a 1989 survey of prison statistics found that Blacks constituted 16 percent of the total prison population (Chigwada, 1991). It is also of interest to point out that African-Caribbeans have been found to be five times more likely to be arrested for assault, ten times for violent theft, and seven times for robbery than the White population (Stevens and Willis, 1979).

Britain's racist criminal justice system, which possesses few Black magistrates, is primarily responsible for the fact that African-Caribbeans, particularly Black males, are said to account for the largest group of Blacks who are compulsorily detained in secure and medium-secure psychiatric institutions under Britain's Mental Act. This overrepresentation of Black males is purported to be linked to negative racial stereotyping of them as "big, bad, aggressive, paranoid, oversensitive and impulsive" (Boast & Chesterman, 1995).

One in five real estate agencies discriminated against non-Whites, and Blacks are concentrated in areas of greatest economic decline (Cross, 1986). Segregation is pervasive in Britain, with Blacks and other non-Whites living in a decaying inner core surrounded by private and municipal areas which are overwhelmingly White (Rex, 1986).

Blacks are more likely than Whites to be unemployed, jailed, homeless, and poorly educated (Rule, 1991). Surveys by the Institute of Race Relations, an independent research organization, have shown that one-third of all employers would hire Whites over equally qualified Blacks without even giving the Black applicants an interview. Another study found that Black workers were more than twice as likely as Whites with similar qualifications to end up in menial jobs. Blacks are grossly underrepresented in areas of clerical and managerial occupations and in higher education (Lashley, 1986).

There are virtually no Blacks in the top echelons of the British Government. The 650-member House of Commons can boast of only three Blacks and one Asian (Rule, 1991).

Regarding the police force, as late as 1990 the most senior position held by a Black officer was superintendent and out of 2,303 chief officers, two were of African descent (Cashmore and McLaughlin, 1991). Blacks are thought of as alien outsiders who lack entitlement to the rights and privileges within the British social system.

Anti-African Practices in the United States

Even though the first Blacks appeared in Virginia as indentured servants in the early 1600s, America was meant to be a homogenous White nation inhabited chiefly by members of the Anglo-Saxon and closely related races. Congress passed a law in 1790 which expressly limited the acquisition of citizenship to White immigrants and in the 1850s the total elimination of the Black population in the United States through expatriation or natural extinction was promulgated. The Declaration of Independence, which stated that all men were created equal, applied to Whites and not Blacks. For White Americans, the inherent inferiority of Blacks made Blacks undeserving of equality (Horsman, 1981). Equal citizenship rights were granted to Blacks by Constitutional decree after the Civil War by the 14th amendment.

Despite constitutional 'guarantees,' the United States has not satisfied the human rights of Blacks and there are deep gaps between American ideals and practices. America remains a racially divided society in which people of African descent are regularly victimized and abused. It is useful to note that recent census data shows people of color moving toward a majority in the United States population. In response to this, social scientists have recently reported on hypersegregation. Similar to earlier times in America's history, Whites are now creating greater social distances between themselves and people of African descent.

America is a racially circumscribed democracy, offering

equality for all Whites and subordination for people of African descent (Fredrickson, 1981). As Andrew Hacker (1992) has astutely stated, "No matter how degraded their lives, White people are still allowed to believe that they possess the blood, the genes, the patrimony of superiority. No matter what happens, they can never become 'black.' White Americans of all classes have found it comforting to preserve blacks as a subordinate caste: a presence, which despite all its pain and problems, still provides Whites with some solace in a stressful world" (p. 217). The reader should not overlook the correlation between the psychological benefits that Whites derive from the subordination of Blacks and the upholdment of White power, privilege, and wealth.

America has historically behaved in ways which reflect a deliberate intent to prevent Africans from attaining parity with Whites. Racial inequality across several important social indicators is the norm for Blacks throughout America. In their defense White America argues that the Black middle class has developed in the last thirty years, growing from one-tenth to more than one-third of the Black population. However, the Black middle class consists of individuals who hold blue collar jobs and low level professional positions, while White middle class persons typically occupy managerial positions. Furthermore, economic recessions and White racism make Blacks susceptible to falling out of the middle class (Terry, 1991).

About one-third of all Blacks live below the poverty line, a proportion which has remained unchanged for twenty years. These Blacks live in decayed areas of America's inner cities and grow up physically and psychologically separated from the American mainstream.

The magnitude of the parity gap between Blacks and Whites is very large on all dimensions and have been worsening. The unemployment rate for Blacks in 1990 was 10.5 percent, twice that of Whites. In 1987 Black income fell $162 billion short of the amount required for parity with White America. In 1991 Black families had an average income of $20,210, a figure virtually unchanged from 1979, while White families' income averaged $35,980 representing a 3 percent increase in purchasing power.

In American society, White racism appears to impact a significant number of, if not all, the human activities of people of African descent. Concerning medical care, Blacks are underrepresented in clinical trials of new medicines and in general have less access to health service than do Whites. Blacks die at disproportionately higher rates from kidney disease, for which the death rate was 2.8 times the rate for the White population. Yet, despite these findings and the fact that Blacks are overrepresented on dialysis units, White men are twice as likely to get a new kidney as Blacks of either sex. Health disparities between Blacks and Whites exist even when patients are of comparable socioeconomic groups (Blakeslee, 1989).

Recent reports based on 1990 data from the Federal Reserve show that 30 percent of people of African descent who apply for home loans are rejected, compared with 14 percent of Whites. This figure may be a conservative estimate, as some financial companies succeed in discouraging Blacks from even submitting an application for mortgages (Nash, 1990).

With respect to crime, Blacks are disproportionately represented among the victims of the criminal acts of racist America. About one in three Black men between the ages twenty through twenty-nine is under the control of the judicial system. These men are in prison, on parole, or on probation. Indeed, more Blacks are arrested, charged, tried, convicted, and sentenced to longer prison terms for allegedly committing the same type of crimes as Whites. Rape convictions result in sentences of 55 months for Blacks versus 43.9 months for Whites, and robberies result in 37.4 months for Blacks versus 33 months for Whites. Over one million African-Americans are in White America's jails and prisons, or could be returned there for violating probation or parole (Hacker, 1992). Likewise, the Justice Department's Bureau of Statistics suggests that as of December 31, 1990, Blacks made up 40 percent of the prisoners who have been sentenced to death. Black-on-Black crime is the leading cause of death for Black males from 15 to 44 years of age; nearly 90 percent of Black victims were slain by Black offenders and the data shows that Black men have a 1 in 21 chance of becoming a homicide victim, and Black women have a 1 in 104 chance; White men have a 1 in 131 chance of becoming a homicide victim, and White women have a 1 in 369 chance (Bell, 1986).

Feelings of frustration, apathy, and powerlessness foster intraracial violence in Black communities. Intraracial violence is a form of displaced aggression, whereas, instead of attacking the true source of their dehumanization, namely White America, the oppressed direct their attacks against Black people. In addition, young Black males living in a White racist society are especially prone to develop feelings of low self-esteem. Largely in response to White oppression, Black youth adopt a dysfunctional "compulsive masculinity alternative." This lifestyle is characterized by an overemphasis on toughness and thrill seeking as a defense against feelings of low self-worth (Oliver, 1984). According to Amos Wilson (1990), the phenomenon of Black-on-Black violence shows how human needs can become warped. Blacks who engage in criminal activity are acting out White America's stereotypic view of them as criminals and are reflecting their assimilation of alien and negative Western values. For instance, the involvement of Black youth with drugs and alcohol is an important variable in Black-on-Black violence. Consistent with the alienation thesis, Leakey (1961), asserted that "at a time when drunkenness was a major curse in many parts of Europe and America, in Africa the laws of a number of tribes forbade all except the very old to get drunk at all" (p. 20).

With respect to other prevailing viewpoints on Black violence, criminal activities in the Black population also appear to be related to illiteracy, unemployment, economic deprivation, substance abuse, and family disruption in urban Black communities (Gary, 1986; Sampson, 1987). For example, when socioeconomic status is held constant, the vast difference in homicide rates between Blacks and Whites disappears. Among other things, poverty predisposes Blacks to a greater risk of acquiring biological injuries that may contribute to impulsive violence. Ramos and Delany (1986) point to the influence of head injuries from free falls and auto accidents in expressive aggressiveness in Blacks.

On the other hand, the involvement of Blacks from low-income communities in Black-on-White violence might be indicative of political resistance to White supremacy. For example, Blacks are heavily represented (61.2 percent) in all robbery arrests, and many of the victims are Whites. In addition to the obvious reasons that Whites are viewed as having more money or items of value, there is the perspective that interracial robbery is one form of racial revenge. For Hacker (1992), the White victim dreads that the Black assailant not only wants money "but may take a moment to inflict retribution for the injustices done to his race. Given the choice, White people would far rather be confronted by a thief of their own race. Indeed, they would be happy to lose considerably more money, rather than face the prospect of racial revenge" (p. 187).

In discussing violence and Blacks, it is critical to point out that the killing and victimization of Black people by the police force have been normative events in American society since the establishment of Black enslavement in the seventeenth century (Cox, 1991). As is often the case, the predominantly White American court system fails to find justifiable reasons to punish police violence in particular, and White violence in general, against Black men, women, and children. Unquestionably, police coercion and abuse of Blacks are mechanisms for the enforcement of an unjust racist social order.

The exclusion of Blacks from positions of power is one way of perpetuating the racist judicial system. Black exclusion has been so severe that the African-American Judge Leon Higginbotham (1992) wrote: "I am forced to conclude that the record of appointments of African Americans to the Courts of Appeals during the past twelve years demonstrates that, by intentional Presidential action, African-American judges have been turned into an endangered species, soon to become extinct" (p. A15).

It is evident, as the National Urban League recently concluded, that past and current discrimination, limited ownership of capital (business, human, and financial), and dysfunctional individual and community behaviors are mutually interdependent and reinforcing causative factors for the state of Black America. Yet the record is very obvious that White America has never intended to share power, wealth, and prosperity with Blacks. The oppressed must understand that it is part of the democratic creed for White Americans to unite in their racial oppression of people of African descent (Terkel, 1992). Ultimately, the onus is on people of African descent to remedy the dysfunctional interracial violence and other social and economic problems which permeate Black urban communities. Perhaps then Blacks will gain some measure of autonomy, as well as political and economic power, in this country.

Anti-African Practices in Canada

In 1689 the French brought Africans into Canada as agricultural workers. Slavery did not thrive in Canada because the economy did not require a large labor force, yet it was revived after the British gained control of French Canadian territories in 1760. England's Imperial Act of 1833 ended slavery in Canada.

The Canadian Black population consists of indigenous African-Canadians, West Indian and African immigrants, and a small number of post-World War II expatriate Black Americans (McCain, 1979). Similar to other previously mentioned countries, the social and political associations between Blacks and Canadians of European descent are rooted in slavery. McCain suggests that the White majority occupies a privileged status in Canadian society and subjugates people of African descent.

This dominant group considers itself to be of superior mental capabilities and social customs which provide justification for their privileged position. Moreover, there is the tendency on the part of Whites to view Canada as a White society consisting of White Canadians; Blacks are not considered true Canadians and do not belong in Canada.

Official estimates put the Black population at about six hundred thousand out of a total population of twenty-six million, up from about fifty thousand in 1950. Massive migrations of Blacks from the Caribbean over the last twenty-five years is largely responsible for the incremental increase in Canada's Black population. Anti-African practices have increased in direct proportion to the increased presence of non-Whites (Brown, 1984). In addition, Canadian society has initiated numerous overt and covert actions, both legal and illegal, to stop and control the perceived threat presented by the growing Black presence. In December 1992, consistent with the xenophobia of European countries, Canada instituted the most restrictive immigration law in sixteen years on the grounds that White Canadians wanted to "keep people out who are different from most Canadians" (Farnsworth, 1992, p. A11).

Recently there have been allegations of links between the Canadian military and White supremacists and other right-wing militants (Farnsworth, 1993). There is rampant racism in Canada's criminal justice system and police harassment and brutality against Blacks is routine. Recent statistical evidence showed that in metropolitan Toronto, Black youths in the age group eighteen to twenty-four were at least twice as likely to be stopped by the police, compared with a quarter of White youths. From 1986-1993, the number of Blacks incarcerated in Ontario increased by 204 percent, compared to a 23 percent increase for Whites. Blacks are twenty-seven times more likely than Whites to be jailed prior to their trials for drug offenses, and are twenty times as likely as Whites to be imprisoned for drug possession charges (Farnsworth, 1996).

These anti-Black practices have engendered feelings of alienation and frustration in Canadian Blacks (McCain, 1979). Blacks have participated in political activities in an attempt to redress racial injustices (Burns, 1989), yet their efforts do not appear to have had any significant effect on Canada's racial status quo.

Anti-African Practices in Russia

By the nineteenth century, Russians were openly advocating the inherent superiority of the White race over people of African descent. Russians advocated the enslavement of Africans on the grounds that only by such close contact with Whites could Blacks hope for self-improvement (Rogers, 1973).

Russian refusal to accept responsibility for their anti-African practices is done on the basis that such an admission would deconstruct the facade of equality and solidarity which they have created.

Robert Robertson, a Black Jamaican, spent forty-four years inside the Soviet Union and could never get used to palpable Russian racism. The Russian belief is that Africans are spongers who look to Russians to plan for them, feed them, build for them, and provide medicine (Adade, 1995). Baer (1970) documents the discriminatory treatment and lack of social integration experienced by African students in Russia who have complained of being called monkeys and of being subjected to other forms of racial abuse. Similarly, a member of the Russian Parliament in discussing Russian aid to Africans complained that the Kremlin had wasted "Soviet resources on peoples who had only begun to call themselves a people, who had just descended from the palm trees, and have only managed to pronounce the word 'socialism' (Adade, 1995, p. 264).

According to Davidson (1992), in the postcolonial era, the Russian expectation was that "Africa, to save itself, would have to march along the "socialist" road laid down by an all-knowing authority in Moscow" (p. 194). It is of interest to note that the current post-Cold War period means Africa's geopolitical and strategic value has lessened for Russia. As a result, Russians are severing their relations with Africa. To illustrate, beginning with

Nikita Khrushchev's Third World Policy, over the past thirty years more than fifty thousand people of African descent received advanced and specialized academic training, as well as military training in Russia. However, by 1992 that number had decreased to eight thousand because the Kremlin government slashed scholarships (Adade, 1995). Haq (1992) wrote that "resentful of alliances and friendship pacts that allowed so many 'foreigners' to live and gain training at low cost in the Soviet Union, the increasingly xenophobic Russian populace now is eager to see the Africans go" (p. 10).

Instinctive Russian racism is now being openly expressed. Gideon Chimusoro, a Zimbabwean student studying at Patrice Lumumba University, now renamed the Russian People's Friendship University, was fatally shot in Moscow during August 1992 by a Russian policeman in order to prevent Chimusoro's alleged mistreatment of a dog. African students who peacefully protested this racist act were themselves attacked by Russian police (Haq, 1992). Such police abuse is only one form of the general dehumanization of people of African descent by Russians (Robinson, 1988).

Anti-African Practices in China

The idealization of fair-skinned people and the denigration of those who are dark and poor are prominent features of Chinese culture. Gao Yuan (1989) indicated that "in China, black is a totally accepted metaphor for ugliness and evil, and people can't conceive of it any other way. In China, tanned, weathered skin belongs to the peasants, who have low economic status, while fair skin belongs to the intelligentsia, scholars, bureaucrats, who stay indoors with books. He who works with his brains rules, while he who works with his brawn is ruled."

Racist ideology has formed the Chinese historical and contemporary abuses of people of African heritage. In the midnineteenth century, the Chinese believed that Africans were naturally suited for enslavement, reasoning that Africans came from the most backward continent and were therefore deserving of their low status in world affairs. For them, Africans were lazy, stupid, laughing, insubstantial, and uncultured people who were incapable of progress (Hutchison, 1975). Consistent with their contempt for Africans, the Chinese felt that lynching of Blacks was justified because of their purported sexual licentiousness.

While the Chinese government has espoused its opposition to anti-African practices, people of African descent have been abused with impunity by the Chinese police, students, and citizens. Meanwhile the Chinese media promotes negative images of Africans as financial spongers on China and as AIDs carriers (Sautman, 1994).

Many of the reports of Chinese racism center on the negative experiences of African students in China. Hevi (1962) provided persuasive evidence on the abuses suffered by the first group of African students who went to study in China in 1960. In several cities during the 1980s, Chinese students, citizens, and authorities used physical violence and other forms of brutalization against African students.

The belief that sexual relationships between inferior Africans and Chinese women will result in the racial pollution of the Chinese gene pool has lead to the arrest and deportation of Africans who have Chinese girlfriends (Sautman, 1994). Whites, however, are viewed as contributors to China's development because they are perceived as coming from developed and prosperous countries. Consequently, relations between Chinese women and White men are tolerated because these women are likely to enjoy a more materially successful life abroad which may in turn uplift their families in China (Sautman, 1994).

In response to these anti-African practices, African students express feelings of isolation from Chinese students and fear of physical abuse when venturing off campuses on their own. Sautman (1994) wrote that "their overall impression was that they remained the objects of scorn and that neither the Chinese regime nor their own governments were willing to take steps to mitigate the situation" (p. 422).

Interviews conducted in the 1990s with African students, business people, diplomats, and other people of African heritage revealed their daily experiences of subtle and blatant racial victimization in China (Sautman, 1994).

India

Black-skinned people, referred to as the Dravidians, are considered the original inhabitants of India. These African founders of the lush Indus Valley civilization, were invaded and conquered by the fair-skinned Indo-Aryans from the North who instituted a caste system which favored fair-skinned people. The very word caste in the Sanskrit language is 'varna' or color. India's caste system was rigid and racially stratified with Whites on top, mixed races in the middle, and the mass of the conquered Blacks at the bottom (Rajshekar, 1987). The historical racist violence of the Aryans and their allies against the Dravidians is discussed in the book by Nehru (1982).

In 1857-58 the British took direct control of India, and strengthened racial arrogance and violence in India. Under colonial rule, the British and Indo-Indians, who consider themselves Whites, were the perpetrators of racial abuses against the Black masses. Since the departure of the British in 1947, Anglo-Indians have been the ruling class in India and their racist arrogance has not abated (Adinarayan, 1964).

Rajshekar (1987) provided disturbing and graphic details on the plight of the Black Untouchables of India. He described these Blacks' exclusion from Indian society and their relegation to the status of subhumans who are treated "worse than beasts." Rajshekar insisted that the three thousand years of hatred and violence constantly manifested against the Indian Blacks, especially those who are considered the 'Black Untouchables,' is "a clear sign that the war between the invaders and the original people of India continues even today" (Rajshekar, 1987, p. 44).

Anti-African Practices in the Americas

The majority of enslaved Africans who were brought to the West between 1443 and 1870 went to the Spanish or Portuguese speaking regions in the two continents. According to Rout (1976), the most striking factor in the history of Blacks in Spanish America is that there has been no appreciable improvement in their overall position. "The Spaniards brought the African to the New World to perform manual labor; 400 years later, this is still his primary function" (Rout, 1976).

Studies of race relations in many Latin American societies document the systematic rejection of Blacks. Slavery ended in Peru in 1854, yet Peruvians of African descent still complain that this nation treats them as if they were invisible. In Peruvian history books, famous Blacks are depicted as being White. According to a Peruvian of African descent, "they gave us freedom, but no land. We never had the opportunity to study" (Brooke, 1989). As a consequence, African-Peruvians' material and human needs are frustrated.

Slavery was abolished in Uruguay in 1842, but no meaningful changes in the racial status quo have occurred for the 180,000 Blacks in that country of three million. Black Uruguayans live in economically depressed regions and hold menial and unskilled jobs. The number of Black professionals in Uruguay is said to be fewer that fifty.

Only sixty-five Blacks have college degrees and there are not any Black political leaders, Black members of Uruguay's Congress, or Black union workers (Nash, 1993). As one Black Uruguayan remarked, "the only time Uruguay notices the Black community is during carnival. The rest of the year we walk the streets and we are faceless" (Nash, 1993). Naturally, these racially oppressive experiences can function to lower and destroy Black Uruguayans' feelings of self-esteem, racial pride, and dignity.

Such feelings of racial inferiority are shared by African-Colombians who comprise 12 percent of Colombia's thirty-five million people. African-Colombians are presently attempting to build Black consciousness and Black unity, and to let the larger Colombia society recognize that Blacks are not in that country simply to "cook and to play football" (DeWitt, 1995).

Panama

Enslaved Africans were brought into Panamanian territory in the sixteenth century. By 1787 about 63 percent of the population in the Province of Panama were enslaved or free Africans (Rout, 1976). Africans were instrumental in Panama's independence wars, contributing greatly to Panama's declaration of independence in 1903. However the benefits which African-Panamanians anticipated after independence have not yet been realized. Rout observed that "Blacks were never able to root out the antagonisms of color and caste." Though African blood is common in Panama, the White ruling elite (the so-called twenty families) has managed to deny Blacks authentic financial and political power.

The mindset and concerns of White Panamanians were clearly demonstrated during the building of the Panama canal in the early 1900s. Numerous Black manual laborers came to Panama from Jamaica, Barbados, and Trinidad in order to work in the canal zone, and White Panamanians became concerned about this increased Black presence and in 1926 the National Congress restricted further West Indian immigration. Shortly thereafter, more manual laborers were needed for modern fortifications of the canal because of the threat of possible Nazi or Japanese attacks. In response, the elite introduced a new constitutional amendment which restricted all non-Spanish speaking Blacks from entry into Panama, but this provision never passed (Wright, 1990).

Today, Panamanians of African descent are largely segregated in economically marginalized communities. Blacks remain underrepresented in the National Assembly and in the Diplomatic Corps. For Rout (1976), "the very dark Panamanian needs both money and fluency in Spanish if he expects to be socially acceptable even to middle-class Whites."

Brazil

An estimated four million Africans were taken from West Africa to build the wealth of Portuguese colonists in Brazil. Between 1550 and 1850 Brazil attracted nearly 40 percent of the Atlantic enslavement trade, six to seven times more than the United States. In 1888, abolition freed the remaining seven hundred thousand enslaved in a population of ten million Brazilians, of whom half were already freed Blacks. Currently more than seventy million of Brazil's one hundred forty-five million people are Black or of mixed race.

In Brazil, Africans experience open and hidden prejudice which restricts their life chances. A disproportionate number of Blacks live in the underdeveloped agrarian northeast of Brazil, an area which has been devastated by droughts. Nearly 10.5 million persons were said to be dealing with the negative human and social consequences of drought conditions, including severe malnutrition and increasing unemployment (Brooke, 1993).

Northeast Brazil has historically lacked the academic and economic opportunities of the Southeast, the most economically developed region in Brazil, where the majority of Whites live. "This pattern of racial group distribution was initially determined by the slave system and later reinforced by the Southeast's official policy of promoting European immigration" (Hasenbalg, 1985, p. 27).

In general, Africans living in Brazil have poor diets, get less education, earn less, and die eight years earlier than Whites. One survey showed that in 1980 non-Whites had an illiteracy rate of 37 percent compared to 15 percent for Whites. In 1980, when 4 percent of Brazilians were university graduates, only 0.6 percent of the graduates were non-Whites. However, African-Brazilian males are overrepresented among the common prisoners in Brazilian jails and are often incarcerated for minor infractions such as failure to possess identity or working papers (Hasenbalg, 1985; Mitchell, 1985).

Pertaining to the labor force, Blacks function mainly as unskilled and underpaid workers. The mean income of non-Whites with a college education is smaller than that of Whites with a junior high school education (Hasenbalg, 1985). Black doctors and teachers earn 20 to 25 percent less than Whites, while Black office workers earn about half of what their White counterparts make. The most recent census data revealed that the average African-Brazilian male earns $163 a month, or 41 percent of what his White counterpart earns. This racial earnings inequity has changed little since Brazil's abolition of slavery (Brooke, 1993). However, it is instructive to note that as in other racist societies, sports and entertainment are the primary avenues in which African-Brazilians can experience any measure of success.

The Black Brazilian political reality can be characterized as one of powerlessness. Africans are virtually absent from senior government, military, and diplomatic ranks, or among decision makers and business executives. None of the country's twenty-three state governors are Black, and of the 559 members of Congress only seven consider themselves Black, while only four are said to be active in promoting the advancement of their race.

Venezuela

The enslavement of Africans began in the seventeenth century in Venezuela and ended in 1854. In many respects, the abolition of slavery did not foster significant improvements for Blacks. Wright (1990) wrote that Venezuelan Blacks live "in the shadow of the slave past as domestic servants, rural campesinos, and day laborers." The majority of Blacks live segregated lives in poverty-stricken areas scattered along the northern coastal crescent of Venezuela. On the other hand, most Whites who control wealth and power live in urban centers.

Blacks are considered to be uncivilized and therefore are

Anti-African Practices and Diasporan Africans 113

said to pose a threat to the orderly development of Venezuela. Since the 1890s, the White ruling elite has pursued the Whitening ideal by the promotion of White immigration and the prevention of Black peoples' entry. They have also vigorously sought to reduce and eliminate the 'pure' Black racial minority by advocating miscegenation to Whiteness (Wright, 1990).

Cuba

Africans played a major role in Cuba's liberation wars against Spain and their efforts contributed to Cuba's independence in 1898. Following independence, the creole elite had no intentions of sharing power with Blacks and instead chose to pursue a policy of building a predominantly White nation. The influx of Spaniards was encouraged and intermarriages between Blacks and Whites were promoted to eradicate the Black presence. White Cubans systematically sought to deafricanize Cuba by among other means, prohibiting African cultural expressions of celebration, drumming, dancing, and healing.

Some argue that after the revolution of 1959, the government of Fidel Castro moved to end the segregation and racism rampant in the Cuban society. Yet, since that time, Whites continue to dominate the highest echelons of Cuban politics, the armed forces, state enterprises, and university life. Black and mixed race Cubans are estimated to make up 56 percent of the population. Yet, of the 125 army generals, only six are Black. According to a Black worker who served with the Cuban military forces in Angola, "the foot soldiers are always Black and the commanders are always White. If you try to talk about that, it is counterrevolutionary insubordination" (French, 1990). Blacks and mixed race Cubans account for less than 10 percent of the leading political and military organizations in the country, with only two Blacks in the fourteen member politburo, and one in the eleven member Communist Party Secretariat (Moore, 1988; French, 1990).

Cuba has recently experienced a large outflow of White

Cubans to the United States and other European nations. Nonetheless White Cubans are still firmly entrenched at the top of Cuban society. In order to garner support from African-Cubans, Castro has made modest efforts to place them in important roles in the armed forces and civilian government. This is a political maneuver on the part of Castro in response to his recognition that the Miami-based White Cuban elite is determined to remove him from power. African-Cubans are said to fear that Castro's removal from power would result in the restoration of more brutal White supremacy in Cuba (Raspberry, 1995).

Clearly Whiteness defines the ruling elite's national image in Latin America. Black invisibility has been the objective of this group. As shown above, several Latin American countries were successful in passing immigration laws to bar Blacks. Blacks made up 25 percent of Buenos Aires population in 1838, yet by the end of the nineteenth century this group was reduced to an invisible minority. By 1930, Argentina had become a nation of European stock by evicting or eliminating non-Whites and encouraging massive European immigration (Helg, 1990).

To uphold the White national image, Blacks are segregated in barrios and remote enclaves. Furthermore miscegenation to Whiteness, such that Black features are no longer socially and politically significant, has been the policy of several Latin American countries.

Many Blacks recognize that achievement in Latin America is heavily dependent on the Black person's ability to whiten himself or herself and have therefore chosen to intermarry with Whites. Many Blacks also mimic the lifestyles of Whites to conceal and deemphasize their African origins. These deafricanized Blacks have accepted the myth of Black racial inferiority. Also, they have accepted both the myth of racial equality in Latin American societies. Consequently, too many Blacks lack the race consciousness necessary to struggle against the oppressive racial status quo.

Instead, Blacks are convinced that they are just as Venezuelan, Cuban, Brazilian, Costa Rican and so forth as their

White counterparts. This leads Blacks to believe that if they simply try harder to become White then they will achieve individual progress and success. Despite such frantic attempts at whitening, the objective facts are that anti-African practices define Latin American societies.

Although the frustration of Blacks' material and other human needs is primarily responsible for their surrender to White supremacy, history warns us that the African condition will improve only when people of African descent put the will to collective liberation before their own needs for physical and psychological security (Bulhan, 1985). It is this liberating political consciousness which will galvanize the human personality to engage in the social revolution necessary for the improvement and advancement of all people of African descent.

Anti-African Practices in other Caribbean Regions

The legacy of the enslavement epoch, and the subsequent colonial period allowed for the economic, cultural, social, and political values of many Caribbean countries to be based on White supremacy—the assumed superiority of White people over Black people. However, the literature is scant on anti-African attitudes and behaviors in this region. This may be due to the illusion that the Caribbean countries are peaceful, multiracial entities.

Caribbean politicians appear to have sanctioned White domination and encouraged a dependent relationship on White paternalism. There are reports that in St. Croix where more than three-quarters of the island's fifty-eight thousand people are Black, Whites own most of the businesses and many hire Whites from the mainland instead of Blacks from St. Croix. On the other hand, Blacks hold most of the low paying labor jobs and comprise an inordinate proportion of the unemployed.

The economic stratification of several Caribbean islands, including Trinidad and Tobago and Barbados, reflects the fact that local and foreign Whites comprise the business elite in these countries. Miscegenated Blacks also tend to enjoy a privileged status over Blacks in the Caribbean (Layne, 1979).

In Barbados, wealth is concentrated in the hands of local and foreign Whites. Seventy percent of the luxury hotels are owned by foreign corporations. Most of the sugar plantations and the manufacturing sector are controlled by United States corporations, while the agricultural sector is dominated by and collapsing in the hands of local Whites.

Local and foreign Whites control the economies of Antigua, St. Lucia, and several other Caribbean nations. The profits gained from the economic activities of Whites flow out of these Caribbean islands to the United States and to Europe (Hector, 1986). At the same time, the Black populations of these Caribbean islands are experiencing severe unemployment. Barbados has a 26 percent unemployment level, which mirrors the unemployment figure of 25 percent in Antigua, St. Lucia, Dominica, Grenada, St. Kitts, and Jamaica.

Haiti

In the mid 1500s the Spaniards began in earnest to transport Africans to Haiti. As is well-known, the enslavement of Blacks was for the gratification of the agricultural and manufacturing demands of Spain. These Africans were the agents of the first successful Black revolution in the Western Hemisphere which led to Haiti's independence in 1803. Yet, since the triumph of the revolution and other forms of early Black progress, the subordination of black-skinned Haitians have lingered on to the present day.

Bellegarde-Smith (1990) detailed how French colonization and the subsequent United States occupation of Haiti facilitated and protected White and mulatto domination. Today, Haiti's social hierarchy is characterized by Whites and mulattos on top and the Black masses at the bottom. These dominant groups' monopoly on power is tied to their links to the West and their promotion of Western interests in Haiti. The ruling elite also have sought for the europeanization of Haiti by violent efforts to disempower the African masses and by systematic attempts to eradicate vodum, an African expression of worship.

The Haitian masses are the most poverty-stricken, uneducated, unemployed, and severely marginalized Blacks in the Western Hemisphere. In contrast, Haitian Whites, who make-up 1 percent of the population, receive 44 percent of the total national income, own 60 percent of the best land, and pay only 3.5 percent in taxes or no taxes. They also enjoy duty free imports and exploit the labor of the Black masses (Bellegarde-Smith, 1990).

The perennial oppression of Black Haitians was compounded by the September 1991 coup which overthrew the elected government of the Rev. Jean-Bertrand Aristide. The traditional mulatto elite became wealthier by exploiting Haiti's political chaos. According to Herbert Gold (1993), "the economy of the wealthy is no worse than it was under the Duvalier kleptocracy. Owning land, exploiting labor, stealing from the treasury or providing airstrips for drugs—it's all just money." The Black masses must never forget that Haiti's light-skinned elite are committed to the perpetuation of racial injustices.

Black-skinned Haitians face racial discrimination and subordination in other regions of the Caribbean as well. For instance, in 1937 President Rafael Trujillo of the Dominican Republic ordered the massacre of thirty thousand Haitians because he was concerned about "the africanizing of his mulatto country." Following this massacre, the Dominican Republic still needed cheap seasonal cane cutters for its sugar industry. In turn, Haiti's mulatto ruling elite sold black-skinned Haitians into servitude for an arranged price of $1.5 million annually (Bellegarde-Smith, 1990).

The plight of Haitian cane cutters who have worked in the Dominican Republic is certainly of importance in demonstrating the exploitation of black-skinned persons in the Caribbean and Third World context. Their plight is another stark instance of cheap and coercible African laborers. (French, 1990; Lemoine, 1981).

The September 1991 coup that overthrew President Jean-Bertrand Aristide drew world attention to the desperate conditions of the Haitian masses. Nonetheless, the United States' inherently racist policies on Haitian refugees have remained unchanged and are instinctive responses which go back to earlier times. For instance, following Haiti's revolution of 1804, the American government banned trade with Haiti in 1806 and renewed the embargo in 1807 and 1809 (Bellegarde-Smith, 1990). From those earlier times to the present day, one thing is clear, White America has shown its intent to oppose the aspirations of the Haitian masses.

Haitians living in Western countries are racially victimized in the myriad ways discussed in this chapter. In addition, by propagandizing that AIDS started in Haiti, the White world promoted negative racial and sexual stereotypes of Blacks to justify the racial subordination of people of African descent.

Invariably, people of African descent are marginalized in world affairs. Our unfavorable status is positively correlated with the anti-African practices that regulate the world order. As I will describe further in the concluding section, the multiplicity of problems of people of African descent have allowed for the development and maintenance of a psychology of submission to White supremacy. This mindset has served to undermine the goal of the collective liberation of people of African descent.

Conclusion

A reading of European history suggests that Europe has never believed in the unselfish sharing of the world's resources, wealth, and power. Human groups can sometimes transcend the past and adapt to circumstances in unanticipated ways. Yet, White power maintains White privilege and wealth, and these are central to the self-image of Whites.

This writer is strongly convinced that Africa will recover its place in the world and contribute to restoring the meaning of life on this planet earth. Davidson (1991) wrote that Africans were once able to solve every major survival problem that confronted them because of the ancient ancestors great flexibility and adaptation. These ancestors developed a variety of sociostructural responses and economies so as to be consistently successful in populating and domesticating even those harshly hostile areas of the continent.

What has corrupted, suppressed, or repressed in contemporary people of African descent the inherent human drive for freedom and to be the authors of their own destiny? Any attempt to understand the submission of Africans to White supremacy must address the interactions of cultural, historical, political, psychological, religious, and social factors. I have previously indicated some of the psychological and historical forces that have allowed for a psychology of submission to become deeply-rooted in the minds of people of African descent. Several additional comments are pertinent to the present discussion.

With regard to diasporan Africans, I believe that careful attention ought to be paid to the psychological implications of this group's removal from their homeland. Further work is needed on the affect of the unfavorable conditions under which the majority of Africans first came to the West and their perpetual domination under global White supremacy.

Although I am not prepared to conduct an in-depth analysis of each factor, it appears that these experiences have resulted in our failure to engage in nation building and nation management. As Dr. Clarke (1991) wrote, "when you take people out of the cultural surroundings in which they originally developed, you take away part of their humanity. African people living outside of Africa are so obsessed with surviving under conditions that they did not create that they often lack a universal view of their condition and how it started" (p. 406). Instead too many people of African descent have reconciled themselves to their oppressive status.

People of African descent are largely unprepared to impose

on themselves the internal changes that will bring about real progress. Blacks have been lulled into complacency because the oppressors have gratified their basic human survival needs for food, water, and shelter. Many Blacks have become accustomed to the comforts of the materialistic West, and see no need to sacrifice for the upliftment of the African world. Clearly these people of African descent have failed to put the will to collective liberation before their needs for physical and psychological security. Yet such a transformation is critical if we are to cease in bestowing this dehumanizing racist legacy to future generations.

Africa has a special responsibility to herself and to her offsprings scattered throughout the world. Until she is a strong force in the world, people of African descent will remain victims of White supremacy and dependent on their oppressors.

Black Africa must break out of its lethargy. Some analysts suggest that the post-Cold War period provides an opportunity for Africa's development. Africa is being forced to wean herself from the Western superpowers who abandoned her after the ending of the Cold War and Africans must now rely on themselves. According to Ugandan President Yoweri Museveni, "The more orphaned we are, the better for Africa. We will have to rely on ourselves. We have to go back to the year 1500, where we left off building an economy integrated in itself, able to produce its own food, its own tools, its own weapons." (Dowell et. al., 1992, p. 46).

Africa must build on the symbiosis between its fundamental values which derive from the respect of nature and life, and the progress of science and technology. African leaders must organize education in order to train the human resources which will engineer development (Kodjo, 1987). Africa must endow itself with a prosperous economy and powerful army. Military strength might be the best guarantor of national independence and security. The military supremacy of the West has allowed its nations to command the destiny of the planet. Seventy percent of world military is concentrated in the United States, USSR, China, France, U.K., and West Germany (Kodjo, 1987).

History shows that nations torn apart by conflicting interests are dragged into degradation. Historians indicate that we lost our independence because of both our failure to form alliances with each other and our military and technological weaknesses. The current artificial boundaries drawn by the West in Africa have reinforced our disunity. Before colonization, Africans moved from one country to the next. Africa must again be treated as a sole geographic space (Diop, 1987).

It is essential for people of African descent to embrace the perspectives of H. Sylvester Williams, Kwame Nkrumah, Marcus Garvey, John Henrik Clarke, and other Africans who stress that Pan-Africanism is the only road to redemption. Among other things, this ideology calls for people of African descent to devise their own goals and strategies for development and progress. This will only occur when people of African descent fall in love with the race and are willing to consistently sacrifice for our uplift. Naturally this will lead to the development of a new self-confidence and self-respect, which will collectively empower us to proactively deal with the interests of the African world.

Undoubtedly, there is a complex diversity of sociocultural realities that divide us. However, this chapter demonstrated that it is precisely because we are people of African descent that we share common trials and tribulations in a world controlled by White supremacy. Similarly we have a common culture and a common geography. Pan-Africanism is the only ideology for the construction of a united and prosperous African world. Our lives will be justified only when Pan-Africanism is enshrined in our daily attitudes and practices. Only then will we become liberated and stay liberated, while recovering our greatness and prosperity.

Chapter V

RECLAIMING AFRICAN CULTURAL TRADITIONS FOR THE LIBERATION OF PEOPLE OF AFRICAN DESCENT

O Mother mine mother of us all
Of the Negro they blinded who
once again sees flowers
Listen Listen to your voice
This cry shot through with violence
This song that springs
Only from love.

David Diop

Culture implies our struggle—
it is our struggle.

Sekou Toure

In the preceding chapters I discussed how people of African descent's dependency on alien Western cultural traditions such as selfish individualism, wanton acquisitiveness, and the repudiation of the sacredness of Black existence have contributed to the present cultural denouement and the underdevelopment of the African world. These values were instilled into our personality structures and incorporated into the African communities primarily as a function of the enslavement trade, colonial rule, and perpetual White domination. There is obviously a need for Africans to be resocialized to their authentic cultural traditions. "The study of the history of liberation struggles shows that in general, they are preceded by an increase in cultural phenomena which progressively crystallize into an attempt...to assert the cultural personality of the oppressed people in an act of rejection of that of the oppressor" (Cabral, 1974, p. 45). Cultural nationalism is a prerequisite for our collective liberation (Lynch, 1971). Knowledge of our past will aid us in culturally defining ourselves, believing in ourselves, and using culture as a tool for liberation.

Nonetheless some writers reject the premise of authentic African cultural attributes and argue that emphasis on the African past is irrelevant to the concrete facts of African existence. These analysts look askance at the thesis concerning the cultural unity of Africa (Appiah, 1992; Hountondji, 1976; Towa, 1971). For example, Appiah claims that "to root Africa's modern identity in an imaginary history—requires us to see the past as the movement of wholeness and unity; ties us to values and beliefs of the past, and thus diverts us...from the problems of the present and the hopes of the future" (p. 176). On the contrary it is precisely because people of African descent have neglected to reclaim the best African cultural values of the past, that we have failed miserably in solving the concrete problems of the present for the creation of a more prosperous future.

The other critic Hountondji (1976) has pointed out that "the quest for originality is always bound up with a desire to show off. It has meaning only in relation to the Other, from whom one wishes to distinguish oneself at all costs" (p. 44). Hountondji (1976) contends that African traditions are no more homogeneous than those of any other continent and advocates instead for the complex heritage, contradictory, and heterogeneous aspects of African traditions.

Hountondji neglects to address the observation that Black peoples' psychological functioning and social existence have been deracialized primarily by the cultural aggression of the West. Hence, the reclamation of authentic cultural traditions can be construed as the quest for the reafricanization of our social structures and personality lives. It is also evident that Hountondji and Appiah have ignored the evidence from a variety of disciplines which suggests that, despite the cultural diversity arising from Africa's complex heritage, it is still possible to recognize common culture-traits in the beliefs, value systems, sociopolitical institutions, customs, and practices of various African societies (Gyeke, 1987; Heskovits, 1935).

There is reliable evidence that people of African descent have similar constructions of their existential realities, that is, their own views of their collective being or existence. Despite cultural erosions, these values have been recapitulated from the distant past to more recent times.

Finally, Towa (1971) makes the important point that material strength might be the best guarantor of Africans' political, economic, and cultural development. Yet he erroneously assumes that for material development Africans must adopt the West's rational approach to the world. It has been well-established that for many centuries, Africa was at the forefront of all human progress. Africa started humanity on the tool-making path and this achievement lifted 'near-humans' to the level of human beings (Leakey, 1961). The reader should also be mindful of the earlier discussion on the historical and cultural factors that might account for Europe's superior technological advances in the modern era. As Wiredu (1984) wrote, "no society could survive for any length of time without conducting a large part of their daily activities by the principle of belief according to the evidence. You can not farm without some rationally based knowledge of soils and seeds and of meteorology; and no society can achieve any reasonable degree of harmony in human relations without a basic tendency to assess claims and allegations by the method of objective investigation. The truth, then, is that rational knowledge is not the preserve of the modern West nor is superstition a peculiarity of the African peoples" (p. 153). He also reminds us that "technological sophistication is only an aspect, not the core of development. The conquest of the religious, moral and political spheres remains a thing of the future even in the West" (p. 153).

Pertinent to our concerns in this chapter are the dominant and authentic cultural virtues which must inform the psychological functioning of people of African descent and the social revolution necessary for our advancement and collective liberation. This chapter is a discussion on the best African cultural traditions of the past with an examination of the extent to which their erosion has mired people of African descent into profound moral crises.

Ancient African Cultural Traditions

Moral crises are pervasive in contemporary Africa. For instance, since 1960 twenty wars have occurred in Africa, which have killed about seven million people, created approximately five million refugees, caused billions of dollars in destruction, and strangled fragile economics. The latest data also shows that the Continent spends about $14 billion a year on arms—equal to expenditures on education and four times health spending (Sheperd, 1992). The Europeans' support of these warfares is purported to have lessened due to the ending of the Cold War. Nonetheless Africa continues to be ravaged by strife, rampant corruption, and other forms of moral chaos.

There is no doubt that diasporan Blacks have also suffered moral crises. Black-on-Black violence, ostentatious materialism, selfish individualism, and disrespect for traditional family obligations keep spiraling in the Black communities of the West. The perilousness of the African situation has been largely determined by the assimilation of alien and maladaptive behavioral patterns by Blacks. Much of the subsequent discussion deals with those African virtues which must be reclaimed by people of African descent for the 'moral healing of the race.' This is an essential factor for the collective liberation of people of African descent.

Traditional African morals are defined in philosophical and religious terms. Believing that God gave them their values, the early Africans saw this as providing an unchallenged and uncompromising authority for their moral code (Khopa, 1980). Evil was viewed as injustice toward God and the natural order which is the expression of God's will (Tempels, 1959). It was also felt that both the living elders and the departed ancestors watched over people to make sure that they did not transgress these rules.

According to traditional African beliefs, moral behavior is determined vis-a-vis its social function and utility. Hence, excessive aggressiveness, undue greed, spite, jealousy, and hard-driving ambitiousness were perceived as socially destructive acts or vices (Davidson, 1969; Tempels, 1959). Hampate Ba (1981) noted that most traditional oral African societies considered lying to be an act of moral leprosy. "In traditional Africa, the man who breaks his word kills his civil, religious and occult person. He cuts himself off from himself and from society. Better for him to die than to go on living, both for himself and for his family" (p. 172).

In brief, social equilibrium was thought to be maintained by smooth interpersonal relationship between all members of the society. Krige and Krige (1954) delineated the ideal qualities or virtues that are expressed in the moral code of the Lovedu of the Transvaal.

The common characteristics expressed in the moral code of

the Lovedu of the Transvaal are moderation and temperance, compromise and agreement, honesty, humility, and respect for the personality and rights of others (Krige and Krige, 1954). Krige and Krige (1954) indicated that they did not engage in the weighing up of one service against another, nor did they attempt to seek prestige by lavishness. The Kriges commented that the Lovedu displayed an absence of competitiveness and lack of force or aggressiveness in their social and political structures. The authors pointed out the marked disinclination of the Lovedu to make comparisons about individual achievements, competencies, and possessions. The absence of socioeconomic stratification of classes among the Lovedu was attributed to this groups' belief that a great person, whether s(he) is rich or poor, is first and foremost a royal relative. According to traditional African thought, the ideal character is embodied in the person who is wise, generous, socialable, meek, and pleases all while offending none (Davidson, 1969).

Throughout traditional Black Africa, the pressure of public opinion coupled with the reciprocal arrangements of the political and social structure provoked individuals to honor the moral code. Conformity to the social code was related to the person's self-esteem and high self-regard for his or her reputation for fairness, decency, and moderation. The individual was particularly concerned with being perceived as wise, generous, helpful to all, and able to get along with others.

Gyeke (1987) indicated that the Akans have a humanistic origin of morality. In Akan moral thought, the primary standard of goodness is the community's welfare, which is inclusive of the individual's welfare (Gyeke, 1987). Behavioral attributes such as generosity, honesty, compassion, hospitality, happiness, dignity, and respect promote social welfare, solidarity, and harmony in human relationships. Extraordinary malevolent behaviors including theft, adultery, lying, backbiting, and fratricidal killings invite the wrath of the supernatural powers.

The Akan's beliefs are shared by other African groups. The Niger Press Agency recently reported that hundreds of people attacked bars and bordellos used by women accused of causing a drought by their indecent dress and conduct. While I experienced some personal distress on reading this news report, nevertheless, I presented this example to show how traditional beliefs in the retributive power of mystical forces continue to dictate Africans' behaviors. In addition there is historical evidence which suggests that our ancestors might have seriously questioned the mob's harassment and assault of our women.

The ancient African had a deep-seated respect for women. Mungo Park, who travelled in the interior of Africa during the late 1700s, aptly observed that "the same sentiment I found universally to prevail and observed in all parts of Africa that the greatest affront which could be offered to a Negro was to reflect on her who gave him birth" (p. 202). Other writers have expounded on the greater freedom, power, prominence, respect, and human rights experienced by African women when compared to their Western counterparts (Du Bois, 1976; Leakey, 1961).

Prior to the arrival of Europeans, Africa's social fabric was devoid of prostitution, poverty-stricken widows, orphans, and unmarried mothers (Leakey 1961; Du Bois 1976). There were reportedly no women without masculine support and protection (Vlahos, 1967). Sadly these social ills are currently destroying the basic structures in the African world. Both on the continent and in the diaspora, Black orphans are growing exponentially because AIDS, crack, and violence have resulted in the disappearance, incarceration, or death of their parents. In the United States, according to the Federal Census Bureau, the numbers of Black children living in zero-families rose from 9.4 percent in 1970 to 10.6 percent in 1980. Future projections are equally grim.

In Africa, drought, wars, and the AIDS epidemic have conspired to exacerbate the numbers of Black orphans. For the first time in Africa's history, it is possible to point to what could be described as severe strains and extreme stress on the extended family system. In addition, the reports are distressing on our orphans' familial, cultural, and social dislocations. The emotional problems and dysfunctional behavioral responses of those orphans, who have been deeply scarred by chronic neglect and abuse, are appalling, as are the reports of African children who have been abandoned to die because severely destitute parents and extended family members could no longer take care of them.

The onus is on people of African descent to cease behaving in ways which preserve these tragedies and destroy the human potentialities of our elderly, children, and unborn. Early life experiences are paramount in personality development and psychological transformation. Black parents' socialization practices must encourage the child to develop into the authentic struggler who lives for the survival and advancement of all people of African descent. Initially, of course, the parent must believe that the oppressive status quo is unacceptable and feel personally compelled to contribute to the construction of a new world order in which people of African descent can become liberated and stay liberated.

One goal of this chapter is for the oppressed of African descent to recognize that African traditions are the requisite foundation of Black authenticity. The authentic struggler is a person of culture. This ideal struggler functions on the premise that African cultural realities of unity, reciprocity, and respect for the sacredness of Black existence are essential to the struggle for liberation.

An important obstacle in the liberation struggle are the conspicuous consumptive behaviors that define the lifestyles of too many people of African descent. Many African youth commit fratricidal crimes for the material trappings of ostentatious garments and flashy automobiles, while other deracinated Blacks are convinced that their human worth is determined by how much they mimic the wanton acquisitiveness and materialistic lifestyle of Europeans. These behaviors reflect the cultural alienation of Blacks from indigenous African traditions. For example, Mphahlele (1959) succinctly observed that the Bantu saying "yours is only that which is in your belly-there's nothing else you can call yours" (p. 112) is diametrically opposed to Western acquisitiveness.

Davidson (1969) writes that "those traits of character which the modern world admires, such as pushing egotism and the desire for personal wealth or power, are precisely the qualities which used to make a Pondo of South Eastern Africa disliked and even feared among his fellows" (p. 68). Our ancestors reasoned that hard-driving competitiveness to acquire personal material wealth above the accepted norm could be achieved only at the expense of one's neighbors. They were further convinced that the greedy individual would be severely punished by the powers of Evil. The Nyakyusa of Tanzania believed that persons who isolated themselves from others, those who did not share, and those who were boastful invited censure and ill fortune. In sum, such behaviors were morally reprehensible and warranted social sanctions. The ancestors' assertions were based on principles of communalism, justice, equity, and harmony.

In short, to maintain social equilibrium in traditional African societies "the ideal balance always supposed enough but not much more: enough for a given community in a given place, taking it for granted that whenever the community grew too large for local sustenance, for the achieved balance, some of its members would find new land elsewhere. This attitude may be miles away from the accumulation drive of our own industrial societies with their drumming emphasis on 'more than enough'" (Davidson, 1969, p. 66).

Another concern is the development of social stratification in the contemporary African world. Traditional African communities lacked the crucial social stratifications which developed in the West. Africa's subsistence economy, with an elementary differentiation of productive labor and with no reliable machinery for the accumulation of wealth in the form of commercial or industrial capital, disallowed for the development of rigid class divisions (Fortes & Evans-Pritchard, 1940).

Nineteenth century colonial rule in Africa disrupted the

continent's indigenous values of social equality. The imposition of bureaucratic rules, which initially placed Africans into tribute-paying or work-providing bondage (Davidson, 1974), helped create rigid class stratifications as did the growth of the money economy which promoted emphasis on individual merit and achievement. Newly formed classes favored those who were economically and culturally part of the colonial order (Adu Boahen, 1990).

Objective status symbols such as occupation and income do not solely define membership in the Black middle class. In spite of the absence of these resources, there are those Blacks who seek psychological and physical separateness from other Blacks whom they perceive as belonging to the lower class. The negative consequences of these schisms are well-articulated by Harold Cruse in *The Crisis of the Negro Intellectual*.

In addition to racially socializing African youth at an early age, the collective struggle for liberation also requires that we dedicate ourselves to the defense of positive African values. Commitment to our cultural development will certainly allow us to perceive the historical links to our predecessors and aid in uplifting us from our moral quandaries. Unfortunately, Africans continue to be pitted against each other for a variety of socioeconomic, ideological, religious, ethnic, and petty personal reasons. As will be shown, the robust collectivity of traditional African societies made our ancestors avoid the environmental and human ills which currently afflict their contemporary offspring.

Communalism

Kinship was the bedrock of African society through all the stages of cultural evolution—band, tribe, chiefdom, and state (Jean, 1991). The neolithic revolution, defined in terms of sedentary villages and the domestication of animals and plants, is viewed as a turning point in the history of humanity and occurred in Africa three thousand years before it did in Western Europe.

One prominent anthropological viewpoint is that the transformation from bands to a more civilized existence in sedentary villages resulted in total tyranny of the community over the individual volition. Sedentary villages were purported to demand rigid conformity because of population pressures on the scarce amount of food supplies. This general anthropological assumption does not appear to be valid for Africa.

One conjecture is that the early people of the South (Ethiopians, Egyptians, and Nubians) came from sedentary and agricultural societies which provided an abundance of foods. As a result, the early Africans had no incentive to aggressively compete for food. This might explain why Africans' social experiences were contrary to the general assumption that sedentary villages demanded total tyranny of the community over individual rights.

The history of civilization in the Nile Valley is the history of human 'domestication' of the river. According to Diop, the form of the Nile Valley demanded that the population engage in a general communal effort to cope with natural phenomena such as floods. The individual, although allowed certain rights, was subordinated to the collective because it was on the collective welfare that the individual's well-being depended. However, though private right was subordinated to public right, Diop's statements by no means suggest the suffocating social tyranny suggested by Eurocentric social scientists.

In fact, consistent with other evidence, Vercoutter (1981) observed that the process of domesticating the Nile evolved gradually and that it depended upon communal action which was founded on equality among group members. He pointed out that the reservoirs built to hold back flooding and extend it to land needed to be carefully planned for the whole country and relied on interdependent efforts. All the evidence, he argued, suggested equality of social status between the different members of the community irrespective of age or gender. His conclusions were derived from the findings that excavated cemeteries showed that there were no racial, religious, or social discrimina-

Reclaiming African Cultural Traditions

tion associated with the burial of group members.

Across the continent Africans embraced the kinship system because they were cognizant of its social efficacy. Davidson (1969) insisted that the endurance of communalism is explainable because it allowed for better conflict-resolution, fostered stability, promoted both cooperation and social unity, and protected the elderly, the impoverished, and orphans. In precolonial Africa, the community took care of those who were unable to earn a living due to personal or physical infirmities, and poverty was virtually absent. With European penetration of Africa, the very poor came to include those who were impoverished by competition for resources (Iliffe, 1987). In short, collective effort was critical for the tasks of life and made for Africa's economic, cultural, social, and political progress.

The evidence is strong on the essentiality of communalism. Fortes and Evans-Pritchard (1940) reveal that the greatest common interest of African society is that "rights be respected, duties performed, the sentiments binding the members together upheld or else the social order would be so insecure that the material needs of existence could no longer be satisfied. Productive labor would come to a standstill and the society disintegrate" (p. 20). Despite the colonial partitioning of Africa, the communalistic propensity of Africans has enabled them to maintain kinship ties and economic activities across colonial boundaries, particularly at the grassroots level. Asiwaju (1985) stated that the African's tendency is for boundaries that join rather than those that divide.

Gyeke has provided a useful definition of the term "communalism" which is worth quoting at length. According to him, "communalism may be defined as the doctrine that the group (that is, the society) constitutes the focus of the activities of the individual members of the society. The doctrine places emphasis on the activity and success of the wider society rather than, though not necessarily at the expense of, or to the detriment of, the individual." He mentioned further that "the success and meaning of the individual's life depend on identifying oneself with the group. This identification is the basis of the reciprocal relationships between the individual and the group. It is also the ground of the overriding emphasis on the individual's obligation to the members of the group; it enjoins upon him or her the obligation to think and act in terms of the survival of the group as a whole. In fact, one's personal sense of responsibility is measured in terms of responsiveness and sensitivity to the needs and demands of the group. Since this sense of responsibility is enjoined equally upon each member of the group who in turn is expected to enhance the welfare of the group as a whole, communalism maximizes the interests of all the individual members of the society. The individual and the common goods are tied up together and overlap. Therefore any conflict stems from a misconception either of the common good, of the individual good, or of the relationship between the two" (p. 156). In other words, collective well-being, interdependences, reciprocities, and individual obligations are moral imperatives in traditional African communities.

Blyden, in highlighting Africa's cooperative spirit, wrote that "Africans living under native laws and institutions would never cooperate with any man or company to the end that one man or company should appropriate to his or their own use and benefit the whole of the surplus wealth resulting from their joint efforts...This surplus wealth is in a most orderly manner subdivided among all the people cooperating. 'Unto each according to his several ability.' Those whose efforts are worth more received proportionately a greater share of the surplus... 'What is mine goes; what is ours abides.' Under her system there must be no exploiters and no proletariats" (Lynch, 1971, p. 172-173). In precolonial West Africa, for instance, our ancestors sought to establish a "communism of industry and for the distribution of goods and services according to human need" (Du Bois, 1976, p. 163). Socialism then was inherent to African society.

The individual who had managed to acquire some wealth also had the burden of generosity. Among the Tswana, according to Alverson (1978), to renege on this responsibility could result in social sanctions such as the loss of services. Moreover, for the Tswana, wealth was broadly defined in cultural terms as "the attainment of the personally and socially necessary conditions for a meaningful cultural existence. Thus children, cattle, fields, family, cultural knowledge, and so forth are all described as 'wealth,' but this is not because some set of exchanges is possible among them. These varieties of wealth are all 'capital' in the sense that they are crucially important to production of the means of cultural existence" (p. 121). In his book *Of Water and the Spirit*, Malidoma Some' (1994) wrote: "Wealth among the Dagara is determined not by how many things you have, but how many people you have around you. A person's happiness is directly linked to the amount of attention and love coming to him or her from other people. In this, the elder is the most blessed because he is in the most visible position to receive a lot of attention. The child is too, because it 'belongs' to the whole community" (p. 23-24).

Our ancestors had other viewpoints on the ideal factors which promote cooperative connection with others and the community. Krige and Krige (1954) reported that "the genius of the legal system is skillful use of the restitutive sanction in its spiritual rather than its material sense. The fundamental objective is the reestablishment of relations that have become broken or strained and that objective is achieved not so much by vindicating rules as by reconciling parties. There is indeed a tacit assumption that the social equilibrium will be maintained if personal relations are suitably adjusted... The primary task of the courts is therefore to smooth out personal difficulties rather than to settle legal issues. For in law as in life it is not the rule that is important but the personal and social relations...As laws and institutions exist for human beings, they are not ends in themselves, and even the most fundamental duties and obligations between individuals and groups are conditional upon the ever-invoked 'if they agree.' If people do not agree there can be no relationship. If they have to be coerced there cannot be genuine agreement" (p. 77).

Despite all the historical traumas and cultural erosions, the modern African world retains the capacity to be the moral vanguard for civilization. Maquet (1972) wrote that "we have already suggested the remarkable harmony and balance that traditional Africa achieved in the organization of human relationships. By various means, Africans have succeeded in reducing tensions and resolving conflicts between individuals and groups more effectively, it seems, than the peoples of the West. The field of human relations is one of the domains in which we believe, and hope, Africanity will make valuable contributions to the common heritage of humanity." (p. 13).

In his book *Mind of South Africa* (1990), Allister Sparks says that traditional African societies were sophisticated organisms finely tuned to the exigencies of climate and environment, even in those areas of the continent which were harsh. He also referred to the fact that "in their communal relationships, and elaborate links of mutual responsibility, with their generic love of children and respect for the aged, they cultivated a respect for human values and human worth far in advance of the materialistic West" (p. 5). In reflecting on the Zimbabweans' behavior after independence, Moore-King (1984), a White Rhodesian asserted: "The truth is that our fellow countrymen have shown us the meaning of the words we once spoke so easily. The truth is that they have shown us how civilized people conduct themselves. We have much to learn about civilized, honest behavior" (p. 132). So, it is possible to agree with Gyeke (1987) when he commented that the "social, nonindividualistic character of traditional African conceptions of the value of man and the relationships between people in a society, and the sense of community and solidarity, mutual social responsibility are in harmony with the contemporary cultural ethos and can provide an adequate basis for us" (p. 40).

There are people of African descent who might find it difficult to fully actualize these communalistic virtues in their daily life experiences. This is due to the fact that we live in a world heavily controlled by European values of rugged individualism, hard-driving competitiveness, wanton acquisitiveness, the prominence of individual rights over individual obligations, and rigid social class stratifications. African disunity is endemic and has been primarily promoted by European hegemony. Many people of African descent are unwilling to disabuse themselves of their own selfish interests and internalize the concept of Pan-Africanism.

In the extreme instance, ethnic rivalries among Black people, which were rooted in the colonial period, have led to destructive civil wars in Mozambique, Angola, Uganda, Sierra Leone, Rwanda, and other African states. While in the West, a psychology of disunity has allowed Africans across the diaspora to fall deep into a quagmire of Black-on-Black violence and other forms of Black self-abuse.

It is important to underscore that too many people of African descent have reconciled themselves to their immoral behaviors. What is just as distressing is that many Blacks see no reason to strive diligently to transcend the differences that engender Black disunity and become united. Yet history warns that only when Black people achieved some level of unity in the liberation struggle against White supremacy were they able to restore and maintain African dignity, liberty, and sovereignty.

African Unity

The importance of alliances among people of African descent in the common struggle against White supremacy can not be over-emphasized. From the earliest times the inhabitants of Abyssinia (Ethiopia) were able to survive because of their solid bonds of kinship which promoted reciprocity, interdependence, and solidarity. These kinship bonds were critical in the military victory of the Ethiopian empire against Italian colonial occupation in 1896. According to Davidson (1974), it was essentially against this highly personal system of rule "that the Italian invaders of 1930s were to strike their heads; not even in the wake of the second world war would there be serious inroads into its all pervading influence" (p. 108). Despite the fact that

Europeans employed their classic divide and conquer policy in Ethiopia, the evidence suggests that at the crucial points in her historical struggles against Western imperialism, Ethiopia was able to overcome ethnic and cultural conflicts and prevent protracted European colonial rule.

In Angola, an alliance of the Ngola with the Congo kingdom and the Jagas of Matamba led to major Portuguese defeats in 1590 and 1594. However, the alliance fell apart in 1600 and by 1603 the Portuguese had captured and killed the Ngola. Despite these setbacks, Queen Jinga (Nzingha) came to the Angolan throne in 1621 and was able to forge an alliance of African kingdoms and successfully resist the Portuguese forces for many years (Gibson, 1972).

On the other hand, Angola's national struggles against the Portuguese (1961-1975) were divided by political and ethnic differences, personality clashes, and Western sponsorship of the rival nationalist movements. Gibson (1972) wrote that "at times it seemed that the efforts of the MPLA's well-equipped forces were directed more against GRAE and UNITA guerrillas than against the Portuguese...MPLA has perhaps killed more UNITA fighters than Portuguese" (p. 223). The problems of disunity were extended into Angola's punishing sixteen-year civil war between the Central government's MPLA forces and Jonas Savimbi's UNITA adversarial forces. As stated previously, the warring factions signed a peace accord in 1991.

Disunity has delayed or weakened the liberation struggles of Angolans, Namibians, Mozambicans, the people of Cape Verde Islands and Guinea, and Zimbabweans against European colonial rule. In South Africa (Azania), starting from the 1830s to the present day, Black disunity has been a prime obstacle to Africans' victory over the entrenched White supremacists. Against the backdrop of centuries of Black factionalism, bitter divisive power struggles between the ANC, PAC, Inkatha, and other Black groups have engendered lawlessness and misdirected political and opportunistic violence in Black townships. The tragic acts of disunity continue to result in the destructive loss of

Black lives at the hands of other Blacks. Only when these Africans recognize that unity is a sine qua non in assuring our victory, will the oppressed of African descent totally direct their revolutionary energies against their common enemy.

Traditional Views of War and Violence

In addition to the erosions of the above cited African values, the destructiveness of war and violence represent other debilitating moral crises for the contemporary African world. Our people experience perverse thrills from fratricidal killings and from other brutal assaults against other Blacks.

Many Black children are being desensitized to violence and death. These Black children have no fear of death because their life experiences have assured them that "death fears no one" (Garson, 1992).

In a world controlled by White supremacy, Black youth feelings of anger, alienation, frustration, and worthlessness, though not the only factors, have motivated them to display various forms of destructive violence. The escalating violence and warfare in the African world highlight the extent to which people of African descent have strayed from an indigenous abhorrence for the annihilation of human life.

The question of human morality and the sanctity of human life was settled for Africans very early in their existence. In the stone age, Africans invented tool-making, however the majority of tools were not weapons. The ancestors used their tools for hunting, wood-cutting, and for other survival and domestic purposes (Herskovits, 1935). Moreover, while Africans were the first to discover iron (Van Sertima, 1984) they did not utilize these resources for the manufacture of military armaments. Congruent with the guiding principle of Ma'at—truth, propriety, reciprocity, harmony, honor, righteousness, and justice—the ancient Egyptian priests, for instance, held the secrets of gun powder and used that knowledge solely for religious purposes.

Some argue that although the Egyptians had long-standing

knowledge of iron, they had somehow never learned to smelt it or perhaps there was never enough ore in their land to make the smelting worthwhile (Vlahos, 1967). Hertz (1970) posited that the use of iron was rare in Africa because metal ores were not found in the alluvial soil of Mesopotamia and the Nile Valley and therefore metal had to be imported. Hertz saw this state of affairs as having a great influence on agriculture, industry, and military affairs. Jackson's (1972) research suggested that this position was invalid. He wrote that "iron and copper mines are found in the Egyptian desert, which were worked in old times; and the monuments of Thebes, and even the tombs of Memphis, dating more than four thousand years ago, represent butchers sharpening their knives on a round bar of metal attached to their apron, from which its blue color can only be steel; and the distinction between the bronze and iron weapons in the tomb of Rameses III, one painted red, the other blue, leaves no doubt of both having been used (as in Rome) at the same periods..." (p. 180).

While the debate ensues on Africa's early weaponry capabilities, the evidence is clear that traditional Africans abhorred violence. Hama and Ki-Zerbo, (1981) explained that power in Black Africa is often expressed by a word that means force or strength. According to these authors, "this synonymy shows the importance that African peoples attach to force, if not violence, in the unfolding of history. But it is not just a matter of crude material force. It is a question of vital energy which contains various polyvalent forces ranging from physical integrity through chance to moral integrity. Ethical value is regarded as the sine qua non of the beneficent exercise of power" (p. 50).

Tempels (1959) asserted that the gift of life is the significant and profound gift of God to humans. God creates, strengthens, and preserves life. Human life belongs to God and therefore its destruction is ultimately sacrilegious. God finds it evil to premeditate the intent to annihilate an individual's existence. Such actions introduce harm to the natural order, natural law, and consequently to human law. The ancestors felt that the community had the right of defense against the perpetrators of destruction and death.

The literature is replete with examples on the high premium that early Africa placed on human dignity and the need to preserve life. Ibn Battuta (1958) commented on the justice which permeated the Mali empire during the 1300s. Based on his observations, the inhabitants were said to show a greater abhorrence of injustice than any other people and their sultan showed no mercy to anyone who should be guilty of it. Neither the man who travels nor he who stays at home has anything to fear from robbers or men of violence.

The respect for life and the human person was such that according to Herodotus, when a Nubian citizen was condemned to death, the state was content to order him to do away with himself (Herodotus, 1928). Relying on Leakey's (1961) arguments, the Bantus imposed the death penalty only when the individual was a persistent murderer. This reasoning was based on the belief that typically the person was motivated to commit murder only under extreme duress and therefore the accused was unlikely to repeat the act. Consequently, in lieu of the death penalty, the accused and his family were required to make restitution to the victim's family. As Davidson (1992) recently reminded us, precolonial Africans thought it better to provide the deprived family with a person to take the place of the murdered individual. He noted that this principle of "leveling compensation was a norm of African judicial practice, even while it must have been often breached in everyday life; and this norm was applied to all situations of imbalance caused by infringements of the given community's rule of law" (p. 84).

It has been maintained "that to the extent that the Egyptians were horrified by theft, nomadism, and war, to the same extent these practices were deemed highly moral on the Eurasian plains" (Diop, 1974, p. 230). African warfare was less costly in human life and caused less property destruction than European wars. African ruling groups were also less predatory than their European counterparts. Commenting on the medieval period,

Davidson (1974) advised us that the day-to-day existence in medieval Europe was likely to be far more hazardous or disagreeable for Europeans than was the case for Africans in medieval Africa.

Chancellor Williams (1976) reported that the humaneness of African warfare was explainable in terms of the Africans' pervasive recognition of lineage or kinship ties. Williams' research revealed that the chief aim of war was to frighten away the enemy, not to kill at all if it were avoidable. Several benevolent military maneuvers were employed to achieve these objectives. Hideous masks and blood-curdling screams were used as the ancestors charged into battle. The defeated or surrounded adversary was provided with escape routes, while the victors acted unaware of these privileges. During the rest periods from warring, combatants were likely to meet at the nearest stream to refresh themselves and laugh at each others' jokes until the drums, gongs, or trumpets summoned them back to battle.

Characteristic of various African groups is the belief that it is sinful to instigate wars because this would destroy the human existence of others. Several African groups such as the Kung and the Tallensi were concerned with conflict resolution rather than conquest and destruction. The Tallensi, for instance, were distrustful of power and the effort to obtain it. They saw offensive warfare as the violent exercise of power and hence detrimental to the moral code. In addition, the Nyakusa felt that anger was twice-cursed, "it curses the angry man and it curses his victim. It brings guilt along with sickness and misfortune. And so anger, say the Nyakusa, must be rooted out, confessed and in confession destroyed, else harm will come to all (Vlahos, 1967, p. 215). In sum, the traditional African emphasized peace and nonprovocation as the ideal relationship between neighbors (Mair, 1974).

Within African village communities, disputes were typically settled by compromise. For example, the Nuers were convinced that disputes could always be settled peacefully within the group. Compensation in livestock would be offered to the aggrieved individuals. Furthermore, guilty parties could seek refuge with a spiritual leader who would do his best to resolve the matter and prevent a feud (Vlahos 1967).

Naturally, there were serious disputes which did not terminate peacefully. Yet, there is evidence which suggests that if violent conflicts ensued, these conflicts were strictly regulated and of limited extent. In his work on the precolonial Congo Kingdom, Balandier (1968) stated that the purpose of violent conflicts was to end disputes which eluded "habitual methods of conciliation." He suggested that in village feuds "...when the blood had flowed—death was not even necessary—peace negotiations could be discussed" (p. 127).

In general, within the African community, the established rules of adjudication tended to provide compensation for the wrong. Among the Galla, a thief caught in the act of stealing was required to double the value of the thing stolen. However, if hunger motivated him to steal, he was set free. According to Hertz (1970), "the Romans whose XII Tables punished the thief with flogging followed by slavery, knew no leniency in cases where distress was the motive" (p. 247).

On the contrary, unprovoked violence against the community called for remedial action beyond the rules. Thus, warfare was an act of reprisal which was motivated by the desire to punish the persecutors. The goal was not conquest. There were taboos against territorial annexation on the grounds that this would upset the intervillage equilibrium. An early African thought was that conquest allows no rights to the land conquered. There were also sanctions against the acquisition of captives and the taking of the spoils of war such as food or livestock because this would disrupt the pattern of community settlement. These sanctions were tied to the Tallensi concerns about the origins of their society and the required behaviors for their harmonious relationships with the ancestors and the Creator (Davidson, 1969).

Changes in the humane aspects of African warfare occurred when Africans became involved with the transatlantic slave trade. One reasonable assumption is that these changes were tied to the relationships between the selling of captives and the purchasing of inferior guns from Europeans. Colonialism and neocolonialism reinforced Africans' alienation from the ancestral rules and regulations that prevented and contained abusive violence in their ancestral communities. Unlike the past, warfare became a vicious enterprise. Even today, the African masses continue to experience the deadly effects of increasing violence and punishing warfare on the continent and in the diaspora.

Anti-Expansionistic Tendencies

A related concern for the African world is that the artificial African boundaries drawn by the European colonialists in 1884-1885 have made Africa susceptible to territorial disputes. For instance, one suggestion is that during the 1960s expansionistic motives informed the boundary disputes that occurred between Dahomey and Niger over Lete Island, and between Tanzania and Malawi (Widstrand, 1969).

Expansionistic tendencies have been expressed by Liberian militants to annex regions of Sierra Leone. In Nigeria's Taraba State, ethnic conflicts have flared because the Tivs, Nigeria's fifth largest ethnic group, have aggressively sought to take over land which purportedly belongs to the Jukun, one of the smallest ethnic groups in Nigeria. The Tivs want to possess all of Taraba State and the Jukun are determined not to permit them to gain any more land and power. In the same trajectory of thought, the wars in Angola, Mozambique, and other countries (discussed earlier) have African imperialistic overtones. For these reasons, it is essential to examine our ancestors' views of such tendencies.

There is literature which largely indicates our ancestors were reluctant to engage in expansionistic and imperialistic behaviors in the early stages of Africa's historical development. Snowden's (1983) research revealed that the ancient Ethiopians of the fifth century strove for a divine way of life, "gaining possession of what was sufficient, they sought no more" (p. 50). Herodotus (1928) was also informative on the antiexpansionistic tendencies of the early Africans. According to his account, the King of the Ethiops advised the King of the Persians "let him thank the Gods that they had not put it in the hearts of the sons of the Ethiops to covet countries which do not belong to them" (p. 153). The Nubians and the Egyptians of Antiquity reportedly were not conquerors. Diop (1974) reported that Egypt only became a conquering nation by reaction, by self-defense after the occupation of the Hyksos which occurred in 1675 B.C.

The ancestors' antiexpansionistic beliefs are perhaps associated with the fact that the traditional African felt that the world was made by God and that earth is a divinity. The person was seen as the protector of the land. The traditional Africans only had privileges of land utilization essentially for agricultural purposes to sustain their lives. The individual could not own land simply because it was not created by humans. As Diop (1987) wrote, "it would be sacrilege actually to appropriate any part of it" (p. 11). Neither could the individual or group buy or sell the ground.

However, Delafosse (1931) observed that the first family to arrive on unoccupied land offers prayers and sacrifices carried out in accordance with consecrated rites. Subsequently, they would obtain from the local divinity the right and privilege to use the land. The inheritors then have the choice of transmitting the land in the same family to future generations.

As discussed earlier, several precolonial African groups felt that violence and conquest did not give them full rights to exploit conquered lands. This was tied to the religious limitations encountered by African rulers in dealing with conquered lands and their original inhabitants. The African ruler recognized that the conquered land did not contain his ancestors and that he was therefore a stranger to the people who held this land and controlled its fertility. If he ignored them, Balandier (1968) contended, he ran "the risk of letting disorder overtake his kingdom and bringing it on himself. He must accept the mediation of the first occupants and solicit the ritual cooperation of their representatives" (p. 38).

For Blyden, collective ownership of the land and its resources is the law of African life. All persons had free access to use the land to hunt, cultivate, and for other similar activities. Consequently, nobody was in want of land, water, food, or work (Lynch, 1971). In African village communities, neither the state nor nobility were more the owner of the land than were private individuals. Nobility also never acquired a keen sense of ownership of land. These indigenous traditions were eroded by European colonialists who introduced the concept of privately owned land to Africa and this, coupled with the colonial boundaries, has exacerbated land disputes in Africa.

There is a definite need to reclaim the values of reconciliation and compromise between aggrieved forces. Africans must become accustomed to respecting the divinity of human existence and be equally committed to the need to preserve life. Africans' detestation of intraracial violence and expansionistic tendencies must become cultural norms.

An associated contention is that the African masses must see our liberation struggle as a deeply moral struggle which will give their lives dignity. The development of this collective consciousness will be facilitated when the masses strongly believe that their efforts will result in positive and concrete improvements for them in the political, economic, social, and cultural realms.

Natural Environment and African Cultural Trends

While cognizant of the European colonialists' exploitation of Africa's environmental resources and the anomalous climactic aspects of Africa's ecological degradation, people of African descent need to acknowledge their complicity in Africa's environmental degradation. Human causes account for Africa's soil erosion, desertification, and deforestation. Prominent among these features are the destructive wars in Somalia, Ethiopia, Mozambique, Angola, and several other countries. These wars have pushed farmers off their lands, made it impossible to deliver seeds to agricultural areas, and killed millions of cattle. African leaders continue to play a significant role in failing to deal effectively with Africa's ecological crises. Ali Mazrui advises that to restore the ecological balance we must restore the spiritual balance to prevent ancient values from being eroded any further.

The natural environment seems to have molded the development of African cultural virtues. Ellsworth Huntington in his book *Climate and Civilization* (1915) concluded that "a certain type of climate found mainly in Britain, France and neighboring parts of Europe, and in the eastern United States is favorable to a high level of civilization. This climate is characterized by a moderate temperature, and by the passage of frequent barometric depressions, which give sufficient rainfall and changeable stimulation weather" (Brooks, 1926, p. 292). For Huntington, Europeans were industrious and energetic because of temperate climactic conditions, while non-Whites lacked the vitality to engage in productive work due to their adverse climactic conditions. Simply put, this is a racist perspective. The documented evidence shows that Africa was the most significant continent in prehistoric development. Africa was where the populations of hominids and then of hominians were the most ancient, numerous, and inventive (Ki-Zerbo, 1981).

Archeological data has concluded that Africa was not retarded by the rigors of the Ice Age. Ancient Africa appeared always to have offered a suitable habitat. Herskovits (1935), for instance, indicated that "when a particular area became too warm or too cold, migration to more propitious environments was possible. In contrast, in the temperate area of the world, the onset of cold weather conditions in a glacial period resulted in vast tracts of land being ice-bound and thus inhospitable to life with only a few specialized exceptions" (p. 438). Writing in similar terms in the late 1800s, Leo Africanus (1869) asserted that

"Africa is a place free from all horror and extremities of cold, because it lieth open to the heavens, and is sandy, dry, and desert" (p. 13). He asserted that while there were certain regions of Africa that had scarcity of water and the soil was barren, populated areas were rich in resources and fertile.

Regarding the Sahara, evidence shows that two to three million years ago, in the Quatenary period, the Sahara was a region of great lakes with high water levels and sufficient rainfall to maintain a type of vegetation indicative of an almost cool climate (Herskovits, 1935). Furthermore, areas which are now desert were once settled in the distant past by farmers and herdsmen. Only around 3,500-2,500 B.C. did pastoralists leave the Sahara (Hiernaux, 1974).

A traditional African belief states that the natural environment and life are gifts of God. According to tradition, the Supreme Creator is in control of the entire universe, and the sun, stars, streams, mountains, and forests are all expressions of the Supreme Creator. For instance, the sunrise may be viewed as God's smile. This explains why, throughout Black Africa, "any worshipful attitude shown toward natural objects such as trees and rivers is in fact directed to deities that are believed to inhabit them" (Gyeke, 1987, p. 76). In brief, the belief in the divinity of nature naturally led to a respect for nature.

Also, the traditional African saw himself or herself as part of the cosmic whole and therefore did not try to revolt against nature or to subjugate it. As Mazrui (1974) wrote: "Of all the continents of the world, Africa has, per capita, the largest number of people who still refrain from drawing any sharp distinction between nature and man" (p. 81). This African response to nature might in part explain the lack of African technological developments comparable to those in the West (Sow, Balogun, Aguessy, Diagne, 1979 p. 86). One recommendation is that we fuse the African traditional respect for nature with our need for technology to ensure the African world's progress, security, survival, sovereignty, and dignity.

Also relevant to this topic is the proposition that traditional Africans were animists in that they located a "soul" in all elements of the universe. Animism is said to blur the distinctions between the living and the dead, between human and nonhuman, between animate and inanimate (Mazrui, 1974). It has been argued that worshipful attitudes toward both nature and the ancestors have made some contribution to animism.

In traditional African societies, myths were utilized to teach individuals how they ought to behave towards nature, how to respect its equilibrium and not disturb the forces that animate it. According to African mythology, "the visible universe is thought of and felt as the sign, the concretization or the outer shell of an invisible, living universe, which consists of forces in perpetual motion. Within this vast cosmic universe, everything is connected, everything is bound solidly together, and man's behavior both as regards himself and as regards the world around him (the mineral, vegetable, animal world and human society) is subject to a very precise ritual regulation—which may vary in form with the various ethnicities and regions....Initiation will teach the individual about his relationship with the world of these forces and lead him little by little towards self-mastery, the ultimate goal being to become, like Maa, a complete man, interlocutor of Maa Ngala and guardian of the living world, leading it toward its perfection" (Hampate Ba, 1981, p. 171 and 180).

Violation of the sacred laws was believed to cause an upset in the balance of forces which would in turn be reflected in different disturbances. Tempels (1959) observed that immanent justice means "that to violate nature incurs her vengeance and that misfortune springs from her" (p. 88). Thus, various African societies use magic, (the manipulation of forces) in their attempts to reestablish the harmony which the Creator had entrusted to human guardianship (Hampate Ba, 1981). To illustrate, the Lovedu of the Transvaal felt that nature must be controlled in the interest of man. For them, "the natural order must be manipulated by utilizing benevolent and nullifying malignant forces, in order to further man's good fortune or to prevent evil from befalling him" (Krige and Krige, 1954, p. 68).

Some contemporary Africans seem to believe that nature exists for their exploitative needs. The trend in the African world towards the abandonment of the traditional reverent attitudes toward nature led Mazrui to conclude that it is as if the dead trees were having their revenge by allowing the Sahara desert to come closer each day. To be sure, contemporary Africans need to more fully embrace an animistic approach to nature if we are to prevent further degradation of the African environment. In other words, the natural environment must be respected and protected to restore African environmental integrity for agricultural productivity and the social, cultural, economic, and political advancements that are expressedly in the interests of the African masses.

Some Ancestral Beliefs About the Europeans

Many early Africans were intransigent in their resistance to the Europeans' presence on Africa's soil. Mungo Park (1907), an early Scottish traveler into the interior of Africa during the late 1700s, reported that Chief Sokee of the Niger was so superstitious that the entire time Park and his men stayed at Marraboo, the chief kept himself in his hut, believing that if he saw a White man he would never prosper again. History has shown that Chief Sokee's prophecy was quite accurate in that Africa has not prospered since the Europeans' began their exploitation of Africa's human and natural resources.

The Kalabari story about the coming of Europeans states that the first White man was seen by a fisherman who was so frightened by this unnatural and strange intruder that he hurried to his community and alerted his people. He and the rest of the group purified themselves so as to rid themselves of the monstrous thing that had entered their world. The Shona of South Africa and Zimbabwe also saw the presence of Europeans as an interruption of God's 'right and natural' order by maleficent forces. The Shona were convinced that 'the ideal balance' could be restored only when Europeans were driven out or reduced to

Reclaiming African Cultural Traditions 153

impotence. These spiritual beliefs provided the Shonas with the revolutionary strength to engage in warfare against the British colonialists (Davidson, 1969).

The Haitian thirteen-year revolution against slavery was given impetus by Romaine Boukman's actions and declaration that the "Hidden God in a cloud is there, watching us. He sees all the Whites do; the White-god demands crimes, ours wants good things. But our God that is so good, orders vengeance, he will ride us, assist us. Throw away the thoughts of the White-god who thirsts for our tears, listen to freedom that speaks to our hearts" (Bellegarde-Smith, 1990, p. 41). Boukman headed an insurrection of fifty thousand Haitians who killed about one thousand French enslavers, leading to Haiti's Declaration of Independence in 1803.

There are many struggles in which spiritual forces have been relied on by Africans to rid themselves of European oppressors. In the eighteenth century, the celebrated magician Anochi told Osei Tutu, who was the first king of Ashanti, that he had been commissioned by Onyame, the God of the sky, to make Ashanti a great and powerful nation. In the presence of the King and a great multitude, Anochi drew down from heaven a 'golden stool' that rested on the King's knees, without touching the earth. The magician declared that the stool contained the sunsum (the soul) of the Ashanti people and that the stool was an embodiment of Ashanti power, honor, and their welfare as a single people. It was accepted by the Ashanti that if the stool was ever captured, the nation's survival, strength, and prosperity would perish. This religious story was used to institute legal rules for the unification of the Ashanti empire. The 'law of common citizenship' forbade the Ashanti people to remember their unique group genealogies or at least not to recite them in public. The symbol of the 'golden stool' emboldened the Ashantis against their neighboring adversaries and particularly against the British colonialists (Smith, 1969).

In contrast, the long-standing humanistic instinct in people of African descent has led many observers to comment on

Africans tendency not to exhibit xenophobic responses to strangers. Davidson reported that the rulers of the Uganda kingdom of Ankole thought the first Europeans they saw were the descendants of their semilegendary Chwezi. The Luo of Kenya shared the same delusional beliefs and they accepted British colonial rule without armed resistance. This was chiefly due to the injunctions that had been issued by their diviners, who wielded considerable influence in pre-European days, against resistance to the coming of the marvellous "red strangers" who were supposed to emerge from the sea. The diviners had foretold of the strangers arrival and the people were advised against showing any hostility to the intruders lest they incur the wrath of the ancestors. The Luo people hereby welcomed the Europeans, fully cooperated with the administration, and generally expected great things of the WHITE man. Some Luo rebelled against the Europeans in response to the message of Onyango Dunde who told his followers that their god Mumbo had communicated 'all Europeans are your enemies, but the time is coming shortly when they will all disappear from our country" (Davidson, 1974, p. 262).

The people of the Congo believed that the Europeans who landed in the late fifteenth century were their relatives. Balandier (1968) wrote that these Europeans were "incorporated into a single landscape, a single symbolic universe." According to Congo logic, "the newcomers came from the water (their caravels were compared to whales) and had the white color of relatives who had gone to the village of the dead. They arrived bearing riches and armed with instruments which demonstrated their power. They came to speak of God and lands unknown. They were going to build the 'society of below' on earth, to divulge the secret of the true life, of power and abundance" (p. 253). The Congolese suffered gravely for their colossal misunderstanding.

Hama and Ki-Zerbo (1981) related the well-known case of the Rwanda king, Nazimpaka Yubi III who, ruling at the end of the seventeenth century, saw pale-skinned men coming from the east in a dream. The king took up his bows and arrows, but before letting them fly he tied ripe bananas to the shafts. "The interpretation of this dream attitude, at once aggressive and welcoming, and in short ambiguous, imparted a special image to the collective consciousness of the Rwanda people, and may have had something to do with the fact that although they were seasoned warriors they did not put up much resistance to the German columns in the nineteenth century, remembering the pale faces in the king's dreams of a couple centuries earlier" (p. 44).

People of African descent must suppress their benevolent responses when dealing with their oppressors. The evidence is clear that Whites' relationship with Blacks has historically been to the former group's advantage. The oppressors have no intentions of destroying a racial status quo which has been most beneficial to the upholdment of White power, privilege, and wealth.

The eagerness of Blacks to assimilate the oppressors' values has led to the cultural and psychological alienation of Black people. The ultimate outcome of Black peoples' introjection of maladaptive and alien Western traditions is the maintenance of our inferior status quo which leaves White power, privilege, and domination unchallenged.

Summary

Lady Lugard (1964), in exploring the achievements of Africans, stated that if the 'civilized' world were compelled to recognize that Black people are the source of its original enlightenment, then "it may happen that we shall have to raise entirely our view of the Black races, and regard those who now exist as decadent representatives of an almost forgotten era, rather than as the embryonic possibility of an era yet to come" (p. 17-18).

Since the fifteenth century's penetration of Africa by Europeans, Black people have been perpetually dominated by White supremacy. As it relates to our topic, it is evident that our peoples' admiration for Western culture led to their disdain and disrespect for indigenous African values. This negative African mindset only serves the interest of White supremacy. In this book, I have provided recommendations for ensuring that we, people of African descent, become the authentic authors of our own destiny. To gain cultural, social, and political power, for the sake of our liberation, we must reclaim and transform positive African traditions for our daily existence.

Clearly the historical traumas inflicted mainly by European and other non-African oppressors have impeded the human capacities of Africans. Yet, the history of people of African descent highlights their perpetual expressions of the inherent drives for creativity, productivity, freedom, and sovereignty.

I concur with Jean (1991) when he argues that "African traditions are not fossilized artifacts in the historical consciousness" (p. 106). These traditions are the requisite bedrock of African authenticity. People of African descent must be reconnected and grounded to the best African cultural traditions of the past. This is vital for the psychological development of Black authenticity and the structuring of our social revolution to ensure our victory in the liberation struggle against White domination.

References

Foreword

Cesaire, A. (1972). *Discourse on Colonialism.* New York: Monthly Review Press.

Fanon, F. (1967). *Black Skin, White Masks.* New York: Grove Press, Inc.

Fanon, F. (1966). *The Wretched of the Earth.* New York: Grove Press, Inc.

Gerhard, M. (1978). *Black Power in South Africa.* Berkeley, CA: University of California Press.

Hord, F. L. (1991). *Reconstructing Memory.* Chicago: Third World Press.

Madhubuti, H. (1977, February). *Education for Liberation.* Lecture, College at New Paltz.

Wa Thiong'o, N. (1987). *Decolonizing the Mind.* Portsmouth, NH. Heinemann.

Woodson, C. (1993). *The Miseducation of the Negro.* Washington, DC: The Associated Publishers, Inc.

Chapter I

Adu Boahen, A. (1987). *African Perspectives on Colonialism.* Baltimore: The John Hopkins University Press.

Asante, M. (1980). *Afrocentricity: The Theory of Social Change.* New York: Amulefi Publishing Company.

Azibo, D. A. (1988). *Africentric Essays in African: Theory, Personality: Theory, Practice, and Research.* Unpublished manuscript, Temple University.

Barker, J. E. (1906). *The Rise and Decline of the Netherlands.* New York: E. P. Dutton and Company.

Barker, J. W. (1966). *Justinian and the Later Roman Empire.* Madison: The University of Wisconsin Press.

Barraclough, G. (1977). *Turning Points in World History.* London: Thames and Hudson.

Bellak, L. (1990, April 25). *Why I Fear the Germans. The New York Times*, A29.

Bennett, N. R. (1981). *Africa and Europe from Roman Times to the Present.* New York: Africana Publishing Company.

Bernal, M. (1987). *Black Athena: The Afroasiatic Roots of Classical Civilization.* New Jersey: Rutgers University Press.

Biko, S. (1980). *I Write What I Like.* New York: Harper and Row.

Bradley, M. (1978). *The Iceman Inheritance.* Ontario: Dorset.

Breasted, J. H. (1935). *Ancient Times: A History of the Early World.* New York: Ginn & Company.

Cabral, A. (1979). *Unity and Struggle.* London: Monthly Review Press.

Caesar (1917). *The Gallic War* (H. J. Edwards, Trans.). London:

William Heinemann Ltd.

Caute, D. (1983). *Under the Skin*. London: Penguin Books.

Cesaire, M. (1972). *Discourse on Colonialism*. New York: Monthly Review Press.

Chinweizu. (1987). *Decolonizing the African Mind*. Lagos, Nigeria: Pero Press.

Chinweizu. (1975). *The West and the Rest of Us*. New York: Random House.

Chorover, S. L. (1979). *The Meaning of Human Nature and the Power of Behavior Control*. MA: MIT Press.

Clarke, J. D. (1971). *The Horizon History of Africa*. American Heritage Publishing Company.

Clarke, J. H. (1991). *Notes for An African World Revolution: Africans at the Crossroads*. Trenton: Africa World Press, Inc.

Clegg, L. (1987). The First Invaders. In I. Van Sertima (Ed.), *African Presence in Early Europe*, (pp. 23-35). New Jersey: Transaction Books.

Cone, J. (1987). *A Black Theology of Liberation*. New York: Orbis Books.

Crapanzano, V. (1986). *Waiting: The Whites of South Africa*. New York: Vintage Books.

Davidson, B. C. (1974). *Africa in History: Themes and Outlines*. New York: MacMillian Publishing Company.

Davidson, B. C. (1969). *The African Genius*. Boston: Little Brown & Co.

De Villiers, M. (1985). *White Tribe Dreaming*. New York: Penguin Books.

Diop, C. A. (1991). *Civilization or Barbarism: An Authentic Anthropology*. New York: Lawrence Hill Books.

Diop, C. A. (1987). *The Cultural Unity of Black Africa*. Chicago: Third World Press.

Diop, C. A. (1974). *The African Origins of Civilization Myth or Reality*. Westport: Lawrence Hill and Company.

Du Bois, W.E.B. (1976). *The World and Africa*. New York: Kraus-Thomson Organization Limited.

Fanon, F. (1963). *The Wretched of the Earth*. New York: Grove Press, Inc.

Fredrickson, G. M. (1981). *White Supremacy: A Comparative Study in American and South African History*. New York: Oxford University Press.

Friedman, T. L. (1990, February 25). German Questions No One Wants to Ask. *The New York Times*.

Fryer, P. (1984). *Staying Power: The History of Black People in Britain*. London: Pluto Press.

Gibson, R. (1972). *African Liberation Movements: Contemporary Struggles Against White Minority Rule*. New York: Oxford University Press.

Glover, M. (1989). *The Napoleonic Wars: An Illustrated History 1792-1815*. New York: Hippocrene.

Greenberg, J. (1993, June 2). Death Row. *The New York Times*, A19.

Herodotus. (1928). *The Histories of Herodotus* (G. Rawlinson,Trans.). New York: Tudor Publishing Company.

Hertz, F. (1970). *Race and Civilization*. Ktav Publishing House.

Hill, R. A. (1990). *The Marcus Garvey and Universal Negro Improvement Association Papers, Vol. VII.* Los Angeles: University of California Press.

Hoare, P. (1828). *Memoirs of Granville Sharpe.* London: British and Foreign Bible Society.

Howe, R. W. (1966). *Black Africa.* New York: Walker & Company.

Jackson, J. G. (1970). *Introduction to African Civilization.* New Jersey: The Citadel Press.

James, G. M. (1985). *Stolen Legacy.* Julian Richardson Associates.

Kelso, B. J. (1992, November-December). *A Legacy of Equality.* Africa Report, 35-37.

Kennedy, P. (1987). *Economic Change and Military Conflict: The Rise and Fall of Great Powers.* New York: Random House.

King, N. Q. (1960). *The Emperor Theodosius and the Establishment of Christianity.* London: The Westminster Press.

Kodjo, E. (1987). *Africa Tomorrow.* New York: The Continuum Publishing Company.

Kovel, J. (1971). *White Racism: A Psychohistory.* New York: Vintage Books.

Kroll, M. (1991, April 24). How Much is a Victim Worth? *The New York Times*, A25.

Lewis, B. (1990). *Race and Slavery in the Middle East: A Historical Enquiry*. New York: Oxford University Press.

Livy. (1919). (B. O. Foster, Trans.). *Loeb Classical Library*. London: Heinemann.

Lugard, L. (1964). *A Tropical Dependency*. London: Frank Cass & Company, Ltd.

Manning, P. (1990). *Slavery and African Life*. New York: Cambridge University Press.

Mazrui, A. and Tidy, M. (1989). *Nationalism and the New Nation States*. New Hampshire: Heinemann.

Meldrum, A. (1991, January-February). Alienated from Africa. *Africa Report*, 61-63.

Memmi, A. (1965). *The Colonizer and the Colonized*. Boston: Beacon Press.

Mendelsohn, K. (1976). *The Secret of Western Domination*. New York: Praeger Publishers.

Moore-King, B. (1988). *White Man Black War*. Harare: Baobab Books.

Motley, J. L. (1898). *The Rise of the Dutch Republic*. New York: A. L. Burt Publisher.

Mydans, S. (1988, January 26). Aborigines Cast a Cloud Over Australia's Party. *The New York Times*, A2.

References

Nehru, J. (1982). *Glimpses of World History.* New Delhi: Jawaharlal Nehru Memorial Fund.

Nehru, J. (1942). *Toward Freedom: The Autobiography of Jawaharlal Nehru.* New York: John Day Company.

Niebuhr, R. (1934). *Moral Man and Immoral Society.* New York: Charles Scribner's Sons.

Perlez, J. (1992, March 17). Zimbabwe Moves to Take Over Whites' Farmland. *The New York Times,* A3.

Rawley, J. A. (1981). *The Transatlantic Slave Trade.* London: W. W. Norton and Company.

Robinson, R., Gallagher, J., and Denny, A. (1961). *Africa and the Victorians.* New York: St. Martin's Press.

Rodney, W. (1972). *How Europe Underdeveloped Africa.* London: Bogle L'Ouverture.

Rose, J. H. (1912). *The Personality of Napoleon.* London: G. P. Putman's Sons.

Rosenthal, A. M. (1990, April 26). The German Question Remains Open. *The New York Times.*

Schmemann, S. (1990, April 29). So Far the German Question Isn't Much Discussed by Germans. *The New York Times,* A16.

Smith, J. H. (1971). *Constantine the Great.* London: Hamish Hamilton.

Sparks, A. (1990). *The Mind of South Africa.* New York: Alfred Knopf.

Sparks, D. L. (1991). Economic Trends in Africa South of Sahara. In *Africa South of the Sahara*, Europa Publications, 31-38.

Stoecker, H. (1986). *German Imperialism in Africa from the Beginning until the Second World War.* London: C. Hurst & Company.

Sutherland, M. E. (1989). Individual Differences in Response to the Struggle for the Liberation of People of African Descent. *Journal of Black Studies, 20 (1)*, 40-59.

Tacitus. (1931). *The Histories.* (J. Jackson, Trans.). Cambridge: Harvard University Press.

Thompson, L. (1985). *The Political Mythology of Apartheid.* New Haven: Yale University Press.

Tucker, F. H. (1968). *The White Conscience.* New York: Frederick Ungar Publishing Co.

Van Sertima, I. (1986). *Great African Thinkers.* New Brunswick: Transaction Books.

Van Sertima, I. (1986). *The African Presence in Ancient America: They Came Before Columbus.* New York: Random House.

Van Sertima, I. (1984). *Blacks in Science. Ancient and Modern.* New Brunswick: Transaction Books.

Welsing, F. C. (1991). *The Isis Papers.* Chicago: Third World Press

Williams, C. (1976). *The Destruction of Black Civilization.* Chicago: Third World Press.

Williams, E. (1980). *Capitalism and Slavery.* New York: A Perigee Book.

Woods, F. (1990). *The Arrogance of Faith: Christianity and Race in America from the Colonial Era to the Twentieth Century.* New York: Alfred Knopf, Inc.

Woodson, C. G. (1939). *African Heroes and Heroines.* Washington, DC: The Associated Publishers.

Woodward, K. L. (1989, March 27). Heaven This is the Season to Search for New Meaning in Familiar Places. *Newsweek,* 52-55.

Wright, B. (1975). *The Psychopathic Racial Personality.* Chicago: Third World Press.

Yeboah, S. K. (1988). *The Ideology of Racism.* London: Hansib Publishing Ltd.

Chapter II

Akbar, N. (1973). The Rhythm of Black Personality. *Southern Exposure, 3,* 14-19.

Akbar, N. (1981). Mental Disorders Among African Americans. *Black Books Bulletin, 7* (2), 18-25.

Akbar, N. (1984). *Chains and Images of Psychological Slavery.* New York: New Mind Productions.

Asante, M. (1980). *Afrocentricity: The Theory of Social Change.* New York: Amulefi Publishing Company.

Asoyan, B. (October, 1989). Racism in the Soviet Union. *World Press Review.*

Azibo, D. A. (1988). *Africentric Essays in African Personality: Theory, Practice, and Research.* Unpublished manuscript,

Temple University, Philadelphia.

Baldwin, J. A. (1981). Notes on an Africentric Theory of Black Personality. *The Western Journal of Black Studies,* 5 (3),172-179.

Baldwin, J. A. (1984). African Self Consciousness and the Mental Health of African Americans. *The Journal of Black Studies,* 15 (2), 177-194.

Biko, S. (1980). *I Write What I Like.* New York: Harper and Row.

Brooke, J. (1989, September 28). Blacks of South America Fight 'a Terrible Silence.' *The New York Times,* A4.

Brooke, J. (1990, July 31). Brazil's Idol is Blond, and Some Ask Why? *The New York Times,* A4.

Brown, A. and Forde, D. (1950). *African System of Kinship And Marriage.* London: Oxford University Press.

Bulhan, H. A. (1985). *Frantz Fanon and the Psychology of Oppression.* New York: Plenum Press.

Cabral, A. (1979). *Unity and Struggle.* London: Monthly Review Press.

Chimezie, A. (1985). Black Bi-culturality. *The Western Journal of Black Studies,* 9 (4), 224-235.

Chinweizu. (1975). *The West and the Rest of Us.* New York: Random House.

Chinweizu. (1987). *Decolonizing the African Mind.* Pero Press, Lagos, Nigeria.

Clarke, J. H. (1991). *Notes for An African World Revolution: Africans at the Crossroads.* Trenton: Africa World Press.

Clark, K. B. and Clark, M. R. (1947). Racial Identification and Racial Preference in Negro Children. In T. Newcombe and E. Hartley (Eds.), *Readings in Social Psychology.* New York: Holt, Rinehart and Winston.

Cross, W. (1971). The Negro to Black Conversion Experience. *Black World, 20,* 13-27.

Cruse, H. (1967). *The Crisis of the Negro Intellectual: A Historical Analysis of the Failure of Black Leadership.* New York: Quill.

Dansby, P. G. (1980). Black pride in the Seventies: Fact or Fantasy. In R. L. Jones (Ed.), *Black Psychology* (2nd ed.) New York: Harper & Row.

Dixon, V. J. (1976). Worldviews and Research Methodology. In L. King, V. Dixon, and W. Nobles (Eds.), *African Philosophy: Assumptions and Paradigms for Research on Black Persons.* Los Angeles: Fanon Research and Development Center.

Du Bois, W. E. B. (1904). *The Souls of Black Folk.* Chicago: A. C. McLung.

Elan, H. (1968). Psycho-social development of the African child. *Journal of the National Medical Association,* 60, pp. 104-109.

Fanon F. (1963). *The Wretched of the Earth.* New York: Grove Press, Inc.

Fanon, F. (1964). *Toward the African Revolution.* New York: Grove Press, Inc.

Fanon, F. (1967). *Black Skin, White Masks.* New York: Grove Press, Inc.

Frazier, E. F. (1973). *Black Bourgeoisie.* New York: Collier Books.

Freire, P. (1985). *Pedagogy of the Oppressed.* New York: The Continuum Publishing Corp.

Fromm, E. (1941). *Escape from Freedom.* New York: Avon Books.

Fuller, N. (1984). *The United Independent Compensatory Code/System/Concept: A Textbook/Workbook for Thought, Speech and/or Actions for Victims of Racism (White Supremacy).* Copyrighted Library of Congress, Washington, DC.

Garvey, A. J. (1967). *The Philosophy and Opinions of Marcus Garvey.* London: Frank Cass.

Goodman, W. (1990, March 29). Color Phobia: The Notion that Some of Us are too Caught up in Color. *The New York Times,* C22.

Jahoda, G. (1961). *White Man.* London: Oxford University Press, Institute of Race Relations.

Johnson, D. (1990, June 4). From Militant to Mainstream: A Politician's Life. *The New York Times.*

Jones, J. M. (1979). Conceptual and Strategic Issues in the Relationship of Black Psychology to American Social Science. In A. W. Boykin, A. J. Franklin, and J. Frank Yates (Eds.), *Research Directions of Black Psychologists,* New York: Russell Sage Foundation, California Press.

Klineberg, O. and Zavalloni, M. (1969). *Nationalism and*

Tribalism among African Students. The Hague and Paris: Mouton.

Levine, R. (1974). Parental Goals: A Cross-cultural style. *American Magazine of Art, 28,* 272.

Lumumba, P. (1978). *Patrice Lumumba.* London: Panaf.

Martin, T. (1983). *Marcus Garvey, Hero: A First Biography.* Dover, MA: The Majority Press.

Mathabane, M. (1986). *Kaffir Boy.* New York: New American Library.

Mbiti, J. (1970). *African Religions and Philosophies.* New York: Anchor Press.

Memmi, A. (1965). *The Colonizer and the Colonized.* Boston: Beacon Press.

Mischel, W. (1961). Father Absence and Delay of Gratification: Cross Cultural Comparisons. *Journal of Abnormal and Social Psychology, 62,* 1-7.

Morland, J. K. (1978). Racial Recognition by Nursery School Children in Lynchburg, Virginia. *Social Forces, 37,* 132-137.

Mosby, D. A. (1972). A Culturological Theory of Black Personality. In R. Jones (Ed.), *Black Psychology,* New York: Harper and Row.

Mydans, S. (1988, January 26). Aborigines Cast a Cloud Over Australia's Party. *The New York Times,* A2.

Nobles, W. W. (1976). Extended Self: Rethinking the So-called

Negro Self-concept. *Journal of Black Psychology, 2,* 15-24.

Nobles, W. W. (1980). African Philosophy: Foundations for a Black Psychology. In R. L Jones, *Black Psychology* (2nd ed.). New York: Harper & Row.

Nobles, W. W. (1986). *African Psychology: Towards its Reclamation, Reascension and Revitalization.* Oakland, CA: Black Family Institute.

Parker, S. and Kleiner, R. (1966). Characteristics of Negro Mothers in Single-headed Households. *Journal of Marriage and Family, 28,* 507-513.

Pettigrew, T. F. (1964). *A Profile of the Negro.* New York: Van Nostrand Reinhold.

Plumpp, S. D. (1987). *Black Rituals.* Chicago: Third World Press.

Sartre, J. P. (1968). In F. Fanon (ed.) *Wretched of the Earth* (pp. 7-31). New York: Grove Press, Inc.

Semaj, L. T. (1981). The Black Self, Identity, and Models for a Psychology of Black Liberation. *The Western Journal of Black Studies, 5,* 158-171.

Simmons, M. (1990, December 26). Anti-Racism Group Aids 'New French'. *The New York Times,* A6.

Sparks, A. (1990). *The Mind of South Africa.* New York: Alfred Knopf.

Spencer, M. B. (1984). Black Children's Ethnic Identity Formation: Risk and Resilience of Castelike Minorities. In J. S. Phinney and M. J. Rotherram (Eds.), *Children's Ethnic Socialization: Pluralism and Development,* (pp. 103-116). CA: Sage.

Spencer, M. B. and Horowitz, F. D. (1973). Effects of Systematic Social and Token Reinforcement on the Modification of Racial and Color Concept Attitudes in Black and White Preschool Children. *Developmental Psychology 9* (2), 246-254.

Steele, S. (1990). *The Content of Our Character.* New York: St. Martin's Press.

Stuckey, S. (1987). *Slave Culture.* New York: Oxford University Press.

Thomas, C. (1971). *Boys No More.* Beverly Hills, CA: Glencove Press.

Toldson, J. and Pasteur, A. (1975). Developmental Stages of Black Self Discovery: Implications for Using Black Art Forms in Group Interactions. *Journal of Negro Education, 44,* 130-138.

White, J. (1970, August 24). Toward a Black Psychology. *Ebony,* 44-45, 48-50.

Williams, C. (1976). *The Destruction of Black Civilization.* Chicago: Third World Press.

Williams, R. L. (1981). *The Collective Black Mind: An Afrocentric Theory of Black Personality.* St. Louis: Williams and Associates, Inc.

Woodson, C. (1933). *The Mis-education of the Negro.* Washington, DC: Associated Publishers.

Wright, B. (1975). *The Psychopathic Racial Personality.* Chicago: Third World Press.

Chapter III

Abubakar, A. (1989). *Africa and the Challenge of Development: Acquiescence and Dependency Versus Freedom and Development.* New York: Praeger.

Adu Boahen, A. (1987). *African Perspectives on Colonialism.* Baltimore: The John Hopkins University Press.

Adu Boahen, A. (1990). *Africa Under Colonial Domination 1880-1....935.* California: James Currey.

Africa Report (1990, June-August). *The Balance Sheet on Human Development,* 5-11.

Ajayi, J. F. Ade and Crowder, M. (1972). *History of West Africa.* New York: Columbia University Press.

Altman, L. K. (1991, July 23). Catastrophic Cholera is Sweeping Africa. *The New York Times.*

Ayisi, R. A. (1991, March-April). The Problems of Peace. *Africa Report,* 23-25.

Barnet, R. J. (1990, May). But What About Africa on the Global Economy's Lost Continent. *Harper's,* 43-51.

Bellegarde-Smith, P. (1990). *Haiti: The Breached Citadel.* San Francisco: Westview Press.

Bernal, M. (1987). *Black Athena, The Afroasiatic Roots of Classical Civilization.* New Jersey: Rutgers University Press.

Bogues, T. (1984, October-November). Jamaica Today, *Race Today,* 10-12.

References

Brittain, V. (1992). Africa: A Political Audit. *Race and Class, 34* (1), 40-49.

Brooke, J. (1993, April 11). The New Beat of Black Brazil Sets the Pace for Self-Affirmation. *The New York Times.*

Brooke, J. (1993, April 9). In Brazil, Too, the Withered Land Cries for Rain. *The New York Times,* A4.

Brooke, J. (1989). Waste Dumpers Turning to West Africa. *The New York Times.*

Bulhan, H. A. (1987). *Frantz Fanon and the Psychology of Oppression.* New York: Plenum Press.

Bullard, R. (1992). Urban Infrastructure: Social, Environmental, and Health Risks to African Americans. In B. Tidwell (Ed.), *The State of Black America 1992,* (pp. 183-196). New York: National Urban League Inc.

Cater, N. (1990, May-June). Slaughter in the South. *Africa Report,* 21-24.

Chinweizu. (1987). *Decolonizing the African Mind.* Lagos, Nigeria: Pero Press.

Clarke, J. D. (1971). *The Horizon History of Africa.* New York: American Heritage Publishing Company.

Clegg, L. (1987). The First Invaders. In Ivan Van Sertima (Ed.), *African Presence in Early Europe,* (pp. 23-35). New Brunswick: Transaction Books.

Cruse, H. (1987). *The Crisis of the Negro Intellectual: A Historical Analysis of the Failure of Black Leadership.* New York: Quill.

Davidson, B. C. (1961). *Black Mother: The Years of the African Slave Trade.* Boston: Little, Brown and Company.

Davidson, B. C. (1969). *The African Genius: An Introduction to African Cultural and Social History.* Boston: Little, Brown and Company.

Davidson, B. C. (1974). *Africa in History: Themes and Outlines.* New York: Macmillan Publishing Co., Inc.

Davidson, B. C. (1991). Africa in Historical Perspective. In *Africa South of the Sahara.* Europa Publications, Ltd.

Davidson, B. C. (1992). *The Black Man's Burden: Africa and the Curse of the Nation-State.* New York: Times Books.

Dowell, W., McAllister, J. F. O., and Michaels, M. (1992, September 7). Africa: The Scramble for Existence. *Time News magazine, 140* (10), 40-46.

Du Bois, W. E. B. (1976). *The World and Africa.* New York: Kraus-Thomson Organization Limited.

Du Bois, W. E. B. (1965). *The Suppression of the African Slave Trade to the United States of America, 1638-1870.* New York: Russell & Russell.

Fanon, F. (1963). *Wretched of the Earth.* New York: Grove Press, Inc.

French, H. W. (1991, April 2). Uneasy Caribbean Islands Warm to Motherland. *The New York Times.*

Gibson, R. (1972). *African Liberation Movements: Contemporary Struggles against White Minority Rule.* New York: Oxford University Press.

References

Hadjor, K. B. (1987). *On Transforming Africa: Discourse with Africa's Leaders*. New Jersey: Africa World Press.

Haq, F. (1992, August 19-25). Russians Reject Ties that Bound Soviets to Third World. *The City Sun*, 10.

Harrison, L. D. (1986). African Sea Forces. In B. E. Arlinghaus and Pauline H. Baker (Eds.), *African Armies: Evolution and Capabilities*, (pp.151-173). Westview Press.

Hill, R. A. (1990). *The Marcus Garvey and Universal Negro Improvement Association Papers (Vol. VII)*. Los Angeles: University of California Press.

Jackson, J. G. (1970). *Introduction to African Civilization*. New Jersey: Citadel Press.

Jackson, J. G. (1972). *Man, God and Civilization*. New Jersey: Citadel Press.

Keller, B. (1992, August 12). A Black in Blue: Taunts from Township's Youth. *The New York Times*, A3.

Kennedy, R. F. and Rivera, D. (1992, August 19). Pollution's Chief Victims: The Poor. *The New York Times*, A19.

Ki-Zerbo, J. (1981). *General History of Africa I: Methodology and Prehistory*. CA: University of California Press.

Ki-Zerbo, J. (1982). *Culture and Development*. Paper presented at the OAU.

Kodjo, E. (1987). *Africa Tomorrow*. New York: Continuum Publishing Company.

Levitt, K. P. (1991). *The Origins and Consequences of Jamaica's*

Debt Crisis. Mona, Jamaica: Consortium Graduate School of Social Sciences.

Manning, P. (1990). *Slavery and African Life*. New York: Cambridge University Press.

Mazrui, A. and Tidy, M. (1989). *Nationalism and the New Nation States*. New Hampshire: Heinemann.

McCord, C. and Freeman, H. (1990). Excess Mortality in Harlem. *New England Journal of Medicine*, 322 (3), 183-177.

Meldrum, A. (1991, January-February). Refuge from Renamo. *Africa Report*, 61-63.

Meldrum, A. (1993, March-April). Peace at Last. *Africa Report*, 47-50.

Morma, C. (1991, May-June). The Pariah's New. *Africa Report*, 61-63.

Nobel, K. B. (1990, April 26). Angola Railway Attacks Hit the Starving Hardest. *The New York Times*.

Ostheimer, J. M. (1986). Peacekeeping and Warmaking: Future Military Challenges in Africa. In B. E. Arlinghaus and P. H. Baker (Eds.), *African Armies: Evolutions and Capabilities* (pp. 32-51). Boulder: Westview Press.

Perlez, J. (1992, March 7). Southern Africa Hit by the Worst Drought of the 20th century. *The New York Times*, A1, A4.

Prendergast, J. (1991). The Crisis of Survival. *Africa Report*, 31-33.

Rodney, W. (1972). *How Europe Underdeveloped Africa*.

London: Bogle L'Ouverture.

Samkange, S. (1971). *African Saga: A Brief Introduction To African History.* New York: Abingdon Press.

Schneider, K. (1991, October 25). Minorities Join to Fight Toxic Waste. *The New York Times,* A20.

Schultheis, M. J. (1989). Refugees in Africa: The Geo-politics of Forced Displacement. *African Studies Review, 32* (1), 3-29.

Seegers, A. (1986). From Liberation to Modernization: Transforming Revolutionary Paramilitary Forces into Standing Professional Armies. In B. E. Arlinghaus and P. H. Baker (Eds.), *African Armies: Evolution and Capabilities* (pp. 52-83). Boulder: Westview Press.

Shepherd, A. (1992, September-October). Dealing with Desertification. *Africa Report, 37* (5), 45-48.

Snyder, C. P. (1986). African Ground Forces. In B. E. Arlinghaus and Pauline H. Baker (Eds.), *African Armies: Evolution and Capabilities,* (pp. 52-83). Boulder: Westview Press.

Sparks, D. L. (1990). *Africa South of the Sahara.* Europa Publications Inc.

Stoecker, H. (1986). *German Imperialism in Africa from the Beginning until the Second World War.* London: C. Hurst & Company.

Third World Network. (1989). Toxic Waste Dumping in the Third World. *Race and Class, 30* (3), 47-57.

Thom, W. G. (1986). Sub-Saharan Africa's Changing Military Capabilities. In B. E. Arlinghaus and P. H. Baker (Eds.),

African Armies: Evolution and Capabilities, (pp. 97-112). Boulder: Westview Press.

Timberlake, L. (1985). *Africa in Crisis: The Causes and the Cures of Environmental Bankruptcy.* London: Earthscan.

Turok, L. (1989, February 13-19). *Debt—The War of Guns.* West Africa.

United Nations. (1991). *Africa's Children, Africa's Future.* United Nations International Children's Emergency Fund.

Van Sertima, I. (1976). *The African Presence in Ancient America: They Came Before Columbus.* New Brunswick: Transaction Books.

Van Sertima, I. (1987). *African Presence in Early America.* New Jersey: The Journal of African Civilizations, Ltd., Inc.

Van Sertima, I. (1987). *African Presence in Early Europe.* New Jersey: The Journal of African Civilizations, Ltd., Inc.

Williams, C. (1976). *The Destruction of Black Civilization.* Chicago: Third World Press.

Williams, E. (1980). *Capitalism and Slavery.* New York: A Perigee Book.

Wren, C. (1991, September. 30). Rebel Front Says it Can Fix War Battered Angola. *The New York Times,* A18.

Chapter IV

Adade, C. A. (1995). Africa, the Kremlin, and the Press: The Russian Comprehending and Communicating the African

References

Spirit. In F. L. Casmir (Ed.), *Communication in Eastern Europe.* New Jersey: Lawrence Erlbaum.

Adinarayan, S. P. (1964). *The Case for Color.* London: Asia Publishing House.

America's Blacks. (1991, March 30). A World Apart. *The Economist.* 17-21.

Asoyan, B. (1989, October). *Racism in the Soviet Union.* World Press Review.

Baer, K. L. (1970). African Students in the East and West: 1959-1966. *An Analysis of Experiences and Attitudes.* Maxwell Graduate School of Citizenship and Public Affairs. Program of Eastern African Studies. Syracuse University Occasional Paper.

Banton, M. (1988). *Racial Consciousness.* London: Longman.

Barker, J. W. (1906). *The Rise and Decline of the Netherlands.* New York: E. P. Dutton and Company.

Bell, C. (1986). Black on Black Homicide: The Implications for Black Community Mental Health. In D. Ruiz (Ed.), *Handbook of Mental Health and Mental Disorders Among Black Americans,* (pp. 191-206). New York: Greenwood Press.

Bellegarde-Smith, P. (1990). *Haiti: The Breached Citadel.* San Francisco: Westview Press.

Blakeslee, S. (1989, January 24). Studies Find Unequal Access to Kidney Transplants. *The New York Times,* C1-C9.

Boast, N. and Chesterman, P. (1995). Black People and Secure

Psychiatric Facilities. *British Journal of Criminology, 35* (2), 218-235.

Brooke, J. (1989, September 28). Blacks of South America Fight 'a Terrible Silence.' *The New York Times*, A4.

Brooke, J. (1993, April 11). The New Beat of Black Brazil Sets the Pace for Self-Affirmation. *The New York Times*, E6.

Brown, L. (1984). Transition from Abroad: West Indians and the Canadian Mosaic. *The Afro World—Adventures in Ideas, 4* (1), 59-68.

Bulhan, H. A. (1985). *Frantz Fanon and the Psychology of Oppression.* New York: Plenum Press.

Burns, J. A. (1989, January 19). Toronto Race Relations Shaken by Shootings. *The New York Times*, A16.

Cashmore, E. and McLaughlin, E. (1991). Out of Order?. In E. Cashmore and E. McLaughlin (Eds.), *Out of Order? Policing Black People*, (pp. 10-41). London: Routledge.

Chigwada, R. (1991). The Policing of Black Women. In E. Cashmore and E. McLaughlin (Eds.), *Out of Order? Policing Black People*, (pp. 134-150). London: Routledge.

Clarke, J. D. (1991). *Notes for An African World Revolution: Africans at the Crossroads.* New York: African World Press.

Cox, C. (1991, January 16-22). Way, Way, Way Above the Law. *The City Sun*, 12-13.

Cross, M. (1986). Migration and Exclusion: Caribbean Echoes and British Realities. In C. Brock (Ed.), *The Caribbean in Europe: Aspects of the West Indian Experience in Britain,*

References

France and the Netherlands, (pp. 85-110). London: Frank Cass.

Davidson, B. (1992). *The Black Man's Burden: Africa and the Course of the Nation State.* New York: Times Book.

Davidson, B. C. (1991). African in Historical Perspective. In *Africa South of the Sahara.* Europa Publications, Inc.

DeWitt, K. (1995, April 18). Black Unity Finds Voice in Colombia. *The New York Times,* A5.

Diop, C. A. (1987). *Black Africa: The Economic and Cultural Basis for a Federated State.* New Jersey: Lawrence Hill Books.

Evrigenis, D. (1985). *Committee of Inquiry into the Rise of Fascism and Racism in Europe.* Luxembourg: European Parliament.

Farnsworth, C. H. (1996, January 28). Canada's Justice System Faces Charges of Racism. *The New York Times,* A3.

Farnsworth, C. H. (1993, May 17). Canada Investigates Reported Ties of Rightist Militants and Military. *The New York Times,* A2.

Farnsworth, C. H. (1992, December 22). Canada Tightens Immigration Law. *The New York Times,* A11.

Fredrickson, G. M. (1981). *White Supremacy: A Comparative Study in American and South Africa History.* New York: Oxford University Press.

French, H. (1990, April 27). Sugar Harvests Bitter Side: Some Call it Slavery. *The New York Times,* A4.

French, H. (1990, December 4). Blacks Say Castro Fails to Deliver Equality. *The New York Times*, A15.

French, H. W. (1991, April 2). Uneasy Caribbean Islands Warm to Motherland. *The New York Times*, A4.

Fryer, P. (1984). *Staying Power: The History of Black People in Britain*. London: Pluto Press.

Gao Yuan (1989, January). In China, Black Isn't Beautiful. *The New York Times*.

Gary, L. (1986). Drinking, Homicide and the Black Male. *Journal of Black Studies, 17* (1), 15-31.

Gold, H. (1993). Haiti's New and Old Rich. The New York Times, A23.

Graham, R. (1990). *The Idea of Race in Latin America, 1879-1940*. Austin: University of Texas Press.

Hacker, A. (1992). *Two Nations: Black and White, Separate, Hostile, Unequal*. New York: Charles Scribner's Sons.

Haq, F. (1992, August 19-25). Russians Reject Ties that Bound Soviets to Third World. *The City Sun*, 10, 16.

Hasenbalg, C. A. (1985). Race and Socioeconomic Inequalities in Brazil. In P. M. Fontaine (Ed.), *Race, Class and Power in Brazil*, (pp. 25-41). Los Angeles: UCLA.

Hector, T. (1986). Politics and Economics in the Eastern Caribbean. *Race Today*, 12-14.

Helg, A. (1990). Race in Argentina and Cuba, 1880-1930: Theory, Policies, and Popular Reaction. In T. E. Skidmore,

References

A. Helg, and A. Knight (Eds.), *The Idea of Race in Latin America, 1870-1940*, (pp. 37-69). Austin: University of Texas Press.

Hellwig, D. (1992). *African-American Reflections on Brazil's Racial Paradise*. Philadelphia: Temple University Press.

Hevi, J. E. (1962). *An African Student in China*. New York: Frederick A. Praeger.

Higginbotham, A, L. (1992, July 29). The Case of the Missing Black Judges. *The New York Times*, A15.

Horsman, R. (1981). *Race and Manifest Destiny: The Origins of American Racial Anglo-Saxonism*. Cambridge: Harvard University Press.

Hutchison, A. (1975). *China's African Revolution*. UK: Westview Press.

Ibrahim, Y. M. (1990, March 16). Bomb Destroys a French Mosque in Latest Display of Race Tension. *The New York Times*, A2.

Kennedy, P. (1987). *Economic Change and Military Conflict: The Rise and Fall of Great Powers*. New York: Random House.

Kilborn, P. T. (1989, October 31). Drugs and Debt: Shackles of Migrant Workers. *The New York Times*, A1.

Kinzer, S. (1991, October 1). Attacks on Immigrant Shock Many Germans. *The New York Times*, A8.

Kinzer, S. (1992, March 1). German Judge Frees 3 in an Attack on Foreigners. *The New York Times*, A14.

Kodjo, E. (1987). *Africa Tomorrow*. New York: The Continuum Publishing Company.

Kroll, M. (1991, April 24). How Much is a Victim Worth? *The New York Times*, A25.

Lashley, H. (1986). Prospects and Problems of Afro- Caribbeans in the British Education System. In C. Brock (Ed.). *The Caribbean in Europe: Aspects of the West Indian Experience in Britain, France, and the Netherlands*, (pp. 137-165). London: Frank Cass.

Layne, A. (1979, March-June). Race, Class and Development in Barbados. *Caribbean Quarterly, 25* (1&2), 40-49.

Leakey, L. S. B. (1961). *The Progress and Evolution of Man in Africa*. London: Oxford University Press.

Lemoine, M. (1981). *Bitter Sugar: Slaves Today in the Caribbean*. London: Banner Press.

Lynch, H. R. (1971). *Black Spokesman*. New York Humanities Press.

McCain-Tatum, P. (1979). Political Alienation: Some Social/psychological Aspects of the Political Culture of Afro-Canadians. *Ethnicity, 6,* 358-372.

McVeigh, R. (1992). The specificity of Irish Racism. *Race and Class, 33* (4), 31-45.

Meldrum, A. (1991, January-February). Alienated from Africa. *Africa Report,* 61-63.

Mitchell, M. (1985). Blacks and the Abertura Democratica. In P. M. Fontaine (Ed.), *Race, Class and Power in Brazil*, (pp. 95-

119). Los Angeles: UCLA.

Moore, C. (1988). *Castro, the Blacks and Africa.* Los Angeles: UCLA.

Morna, C. L. (1991, May-June). The Pariah's New. *Africa Report,* 28-30.

Motley, J. L. (1898). *The Rise of the Dutch Republic.* New York: A. L. Burt Publishers.

Nash, N. (1993, May 7). Uruguay Is on Notice: Blacks Want Recognition. *The New York Times,* A4.

Nash, N. (1990, May 17). Panel told of Racial Bias in Lending. *The New York Times,* A18.

Nehru, J. (1982). *Glimpses of World History.* New Delhi: Jawaharlal Nehru Memorial Fund.

Oliver, W. (1984). Black Males and the Tough Guy Image: A Dysfunctional Compensatory Adaptation. *The Western Journal of Black Studies, 8,* 191-203.

Opitz, M., Oguntoye, K. and Schultz, D. (1992). *Showing Our Colors: Afro-German Women Speak Out.* MA: University of Massachusetts Press.

Protzman, F. (1992, August 26). German Neo-Nazis Firebomb Foreigners' Housing. *The New York Times,* A3.

Rajshekar, V. T. (1987). *Dalit: The Black Untouchables of India.* Atlanta: Clarity Press.

Ramos, S. M. and Delany, H. M. (1986). Freefalls from Heights: A Persistent Urban Problem. *Journal of the National*

Medical Association, 78, 111-115.

Raspberry, W. (1995, June 6). Black Cubans Prefer Castro to Racist Past. *The Times Union*, A11.

Rex, J. (1986). The Heritage of Slavery and Social Disadvantage. In C. Brock (Ed.). *The Caribbean in Europe: Aspect of the West Indian Experience in Britain, France, and the Netherlands*, (pp. 111-136). London: Frank Cass.

Riding, A. (1990, July 5). Spain Frets a Bit as Third World Sweeps In. *The New York Times*, A4.

Robinson, R. (1988). *Black on Red: My 44 Years Inside the Soviet Union*. Acropolis Books Ltd.

Rogers, J. A. (1973). Racism and Russian Revolutionists Race, XIV.3, 279-289.

Rout, L. (1976). *The African Experience in Spanish America: 1502 to the Present Day*. New York: Cambridge University Press.

Rule, S. (1991, March 31). Black Britons Speak of a Motherland that Looks Upon Them as Outcasts. *The New York Times*, A10.

Sampson, R. J. (1987). Urban Black Violence: The Effect of Male Joblessness and Family Disruption. *American Journal of Sociology, 93*, 348-382.

Sautman, B. (1994). Anti-black Racism in Post-Mao China. *The China Quarterly, 138*, 413-437.

Schmidt, W. (1991, November 2). Britain Proposes Curbs on Refugee Flow. *The New York Times*, A3.

Schmidt, W. (1992, August 20). British Racial Attacks Grow, Alarming Minorities. *The New York Times*, A3.

Sciolino, E. (1990, November 6). Friends as Ambassadors: How Much is Too Much?. *The New York Times.*

Simmons, M. (1990, December 26). Anti-Racism Group Aids 'New French'. *The New York Times*, A1 & A26.

Stevens, P. and Willis, C. F. (1979). *Race, Crime and Arrests. Home Office Research Study 58*, London: HMSO.

Terry, D. (1991, December 10). Cuts in Public Jobs May Hurt Blacks Most. *The New York Times*, A1 & A26.

Terkel, S. (1992). *Race: How Blacks and Whites Think and and Feel About the American Obsession.* New York: The New Press.

Wilson, A. (1990). *Black-on-Black Violence: The Psycho-dynamics of Black Self-Hatred.* New York: Afrikan World Infosystems.

Wright, W. R. (1990). *Cafe con Leche: Race, Class, and National Image in Venezuela.* Austin: University of Texas Press.

Chapter V

Adu Boahen, A. (1990). The Abridged Edition of General History of Africa VII. *Africa under Colonial Domination 1880-1935.* California: James Currey.

Africanus, L. (1869). *The History and Description of Africa. Vol. I.* New York: Burt Franklin Publisher.

Alverson, H. (1978). *Mind in the Heart of Darkness. Value and*

Self Identity Among the Tswana of Southern Africa. New Haven: Yale University Press.

Appiah, K. A. (1992). *In My Father's House. Africa in the Philosophy of Culture.* New York: Oxford University Press.

Asiwaju, A. I. (1985). *Partitioned Africans: Ethnic Relations Across Africa's International Boundaries 1884-1984.* London: C. Hurst & Company.

Battuta, Ibn. (1958). *The Travels of Ibn Battuta Vol. I.* London: Cambridge University Press.

Balandier, G. (1968). *Daily Life in the Kingdom of the Kongo: From the Sixteenth to the Eighteenth Century.* New York: Pantheon Books.

Bellegarde-Smith, P. (1990). *Haiti: The Breached Citadel.* San Francisco: Westview Press.

Brooks, C. E. P. (1926). Climate Through The Ages. Second revised edition, published in 1970. New York: Dover Publications, Inc.

Busia, K. A. (1954). The Ashanti of the Gold Coast. In D. Forde (Ed.), *African Worlds: Studies in the Cosmological Ideas and Social Values of African Peoples,* (pp. 190-209). London: Oxford University Press.

Cabral, A. (1974). National Liberation and Culture. *Transition, 45,* 9(i), 12-17.

Chinweizu. (1975). *The West and the Rest of Us.* New York: Random House.

Cruse, H. (1967). *The Crisis of the Negro Intellectual: A*

Historical Analysis of the Failure of Black Leadership. New York: Quill.

Dalzel, A. (1967). *The History of the Dahomey: An Inland Kingdom of Africa.* London: Frank Cass & Co. Ltd.

Davidson, B. (1992). *The Black Man's Burden: Africa and the Curse of the Nation-State.* New York: Times Books.

Davidson, B. (1974). *Africa in History: Themes and Outlines.* New York: MacMillan Publishing Co., Inc.

Davidson, B. (1969). *The African Genius: An Introduction of African Cultural and Social History.* Boston: Little John and Company.

Delafosse, M. (1931). *Negroes of Africa.* Washington, DC: Associated Publishers, Inc.

Diop, C. A. (1987). *Precolonial Black Africa.* New York: Lawrence Hill Books.

Diop, C. A. (1974). *The African Origins of Civilization: Myth or Reality.* Westport: Lawrence Hill & Company.

Du Bois, W. E. B. (1976). *The World and Africa.* New York: Kraus-Thomson Organization Limited.

Fage, J. D. and Oliver, R. A. (1970). *Papers in African Prehistory.* New York: Cambridge University Press.

Faure, H. (1981). Chronological Framework: African Pluvial and Glacial Epochs. In J. Ki-Zerbo (Ed.), *General History of Africa I: Methodology and African Prehistory,* (pp. 371-399). London: Heinemann Educational Books.

Fortes, M. and Evans-Pritchard, E. E. (1940). *African Political Systems.* New York: Oxford University Press.

Garson, P. (1992). The Gun Culture. *Africa Report, 37* (4), 58-61.

Gibson, R. (1972). *African Liberation Movements: Contemporary Struggles Against White Minority Rule.* New York: Oxford University Press.

Glantz, M. (1987). Drought and Economic Development in Sub-Saharan Africa. In Michael Glantz (Ed.), *Drought and Hunger in Africa: Denying Famine in Africa,* (pp. 37-58). New York: Cambridge University Press.

Gyeke, K. (1987). *An Essay on African Philosophical Thought.* The Akan Conceptual Scheme. New York: Cambridge University Press.

Hama, B. and Ki-Zerbo, J. (1981). The Place of History in African Society. In J. Ki-Zerbo (Ed.), *General History of Africa I: Methodology and African Prehistory,* (pp. 166-205). London: Heinemann Educational Books.

Hampate Ba, A. (1981). The Living Tradition. In J. Ki-Zerbo (Ed.), *General History of Africa I: Methodology and African Prehistory,* (pp. 166-205). London: Heinemann Educational Books.

Herodotus. (1928). *The Histories of Herodotus.* Trans. G. Rawlinson. New York: Tudor Publishing Company.

Herskovits, M. (1935). *A Handbook of Social Psychology.* Mass: Clark University Press.

Hertz, F. (1970). *Race and Civilization.* U.S.A. Ktav Publishing House.

Hiernaux, J. (1974). *The People of Africa*. New York: Charles Scribner's Sons.

Hountondji, P. (1976). *African Reality: Myth and Reality*. Indiana University Press.

Huntington, E. (1915). *Civilization and Climate*. Reprinted 1971. Hamden, Connecticut: The Shoe String Press.

Iliffe, J. (1987). *The African Poor*. New York: Cambridge University Press.

Jackson, J. G. (1972). *Man, God, and Civilization*. New Jersey: Citadel Press.

Jean, C. M. (1991). *Behind the Eurocentric Veils: The Search for African Realities*. Amherst: The University of Massachusetts Press.

Khopa, B. (1980). *The African Personality*. New York: United Nations Publication.

Ki-Zerbo, J. (1981). The Interdisciplinary Methods Adopted in this Study. In J. Ki-Zerbo (Ed.). *General History of Africa I: Methodology and African Prehistory*, (pp. 54-71). London: Heinemann Educational Books.

Krige, J. D. and Krige, E. J. (1954). The Lovedu of the Transvaal. In D. Forde (Ed.), *African Worlds: Studies in the Cosmological Ideas and Social Values of African Peoples*, (pp. 55-82). London: Oxford University Press.

Leakey, L. S. B. (1961). *The Progress and Evolution of Man In Africa*. London: Oxford University Press.

Little, K. (1954). The Mende in Sierra Leone. In D. Forde (Ed.),

African Worlds: Studies in the Cosmological Ideas and Social Values of African Peoples, (pp. 111-137). London: Oxford University Press.

Lugard, L. (1964). *A Tropical Dependency.* London: Frank Cass & Company, Ltd.

Lynch, H. R. (1971). *Black Spokesman: Selected Published Writings of Edward Wilmot Blyden.* New York: Humanities Press.

Mair, L. (1974). *African Societies.* London: Cambridge University Press.

Maquet, J. J. (1972). *Africanity: The Cultural Unity of Black Africa.* New York: Oxford University Press.

Mazrui, A. (1974). *World Culture and the Black Experience.* Seattle: University of Washington Press.

Moore-King, B. (1988). *White Man Black War.* Harare: Baobab Books.

Mphahlele, E. (1959). *Old Africa Rediscovered.* London: Gollancz Ltd.

Noble, K. (1992, August 5). Dawn Brings Death: One More Day of Ethnic War. *The New York Times,* A4.

Park, Mungo. (1907). *Travels of Mungo Park.* Edited by Ronald Miller. London: E. P. Dutton & Company.

Sheperd, A. (1992). War or Peace?. *Africa Report, 3* (3), 40-42.

Smith, E. (1969). *The Golden Stool.* Chicago: Afro-American Press.

References

Snowden, F. (1983). *Before Color Prejudice: The Ancient View of Blacks.* Cambridge: Harvard University Press.

Some, Malidoma. (1994). *Of Water and the Spirit: Ritual, Magic, and Initiation in the Life of an African Shaman.* New York: G. P. Putnam's Sons.

Sow, A., Balogun, O., Aguessy, H. and Diagne, P. (1979). *Introduction to African Culture: General Aspects.* France: UNESCO.

Sparks, A. (1990). *The Mind of South Africa.* New York: Alfred Knopf.

Tempels, P. (1959). *Bantu Philosophy.* Paris: Presence Africaine.

Towa, M. (1971). *Essai Sur la Problematique Philosophique dans l'Afrique Actuelle.* Yaoude: Editions Cle.

Van Sertima, I. (1984). *Blacks in Science: Ancient and Modern.* New Brunswick: Transaction Books.

Vercoutter, J. (1981). Discovery and Diffusion of Metals and Development of Social Systems up to the Fifth Century before our Era. In J. Ki-Zerbo (Ed.), *General History of Africa I: Methodology and African Prehistory,* (pp. 706-729). London: Heinemann Educational Books, Ltd.

Vlahos, O. (1967). *African Beginnings.* New York: Viking Press.

Widstrand, C. G. (1969). *African Boundary Problems.* Uppsala: The Scandinavian Institute of African Studies.

Williams, C. (1976). *The Destruction of Black Civilization.* Chicago: Third World Press.

Wiredu, J. E. (1984). How not to Compare African Thought with Western Thought. In Richard Wright (Ed.), *African Philosophy*, 3rd ed. MD: University Press of America.

Index

A
Aborigines, 23
Abubakar, 82-83
Acquisitiveness, 132
Adade, 106
Adinarayan, S. P., 108
Adu Boahen, A.
    on armies in colonial Africa, 74-75
    on colonial destruction of African economies, 71
    on the isolation of African powers, 18
    on the origins of social class in Africa, 133
Africa
    AIDS in, 84
    animism in ancient, 150-151
    antiexpansionist practices in ancient, 145
    armies in colonial, 74-75
    boundary problems in, 72, 146
    civil wars in, 139
    contemporary conditions in, 78-79
    contributions of to human development, 67
    current fragmentation of, 72-73
    debilitating internal factors in, 77-78
    debt crisis in, 87-89
    deforestation in, 81, 148
    disunity of, 70, 121
    environmental degradation of, 148-152
    ethnic conflicts in, 139, 146
    expropriation of by Europeans, 21-23
    food crisis in, 79-83
    future of, 120-121
    health crisis in, 83-85

    human dignity in early, 143
    infant mortality in, 84
    invasions of by Europeans, 68
    as leader in human progress, 126
    marginalization of, 67-90
    military strength of, 121
    need for rural agricultural development in, 82
    negative consequences of trade with Europe, 69
    partitioning of, 72
    personal safety in medieval, 143-144
    shortcomings of Black ruling elite, 73-74
    social stratification in contemporary, 132
    territorial disputes in, 146
    toxic waste disposal in, 85-86
    unity in, 139-140
    water resources in, 81-82
African-Americans
    on death row, 100-101
    mortality rates of, 100,101
    in prison, 100-101
    unemployment of, 99
    and intraracial violence, 101
African National Congress (ANC), 140
African students
    in China, 107
    in Russia, 105-106
African traditions and heritage, 127-139
    about communalism, 133-139
    about lying, 128
    about the sanctity of life, 141
    about war and violence, 141-146
    homogeneity of, 125
    socialism, 136
Africanus, Leo, 149-150
Afrikaners
    ancestral roots of White, 8

Index

enslavement of Xhosa by, 37
individuality of early, 25
murder of Xhosa by, 22
perpetuation of White Supremacy by Boer, 9
Afrocentricity (Asante), 50
AIDS, 84
   and African orphans, 130-131
   in China, 107
   propaganda about origins of, 118
Ajayi, 77
Akans, the, 129
Akbar, N., 38
Akhenaton (Egyptian pharaoh), 67
Altman, L. K., 83
Alverson, H., 136-137
Anger
   Nyakusa belief about, 144
Angola, 75
   environmental degradation of war in, 148-149
   food crisis in, 79-80
   infant mortality in, 84
   living conditions in, 79
   Portuguese colonial rule of, 140
Anguilla, 75
Animism, 150-151
Ankole, 154
Anochi, 153
Anti-African practices
   by Arabs, 3
   in Brazil, 111-112
   in Canada, 103-105
   on Caribbean islands, 113-118
   in China, 106-108
   in Columbia, 110
   in Cuba, 113-114
   in Europe, 93-95

in Germany, 94-95
in Great Britain, 95-98
in Haiti, 116-118
in India, 108-109
in Latin America, 109-118
in Panama, 110-111
in Peru, 109
in Russia, 105-106
in St. Croix, 115-116
in South America, 109-110, 111-113
in the United States, 98-103
in Uruguay, 109-110
Antiexpansionist tendencies in ancient Africa, 145-148
religious reasons for, 147-148
Antigua, 116
Appiah, Kwame A., 125
Arabs
invasion of Africa by, 3
Argentina, 114
Aristide, Jean-Bertrand, 117, 118
Aristotle, 67
Arrest and imprisonment of Blacks
in Great Britain, 97
in the United States, 100-102
Asante, Molefi
Afrocentricity: The Theory of Social Change, 50
on consistency with the Afrocentric point of view, 62
Asantewa, Yaa, 59
Ashantis, the, 17
Asiwaju, A. I., 135
Australia
British and Aborigines in, 23
Authentic strugglers, 58-60
and African culture, 58
and consciousness of the Manichean world, 59
and dedication to African self, 58

and dedication to cause, 60
and familiarity with Black literature, 62
need for African leaders to be, 89-90
and need to reclaim African culture, 61
transition from nonideal to, 61-62
unpredictability of, 59
Ayisi, R. A., 80
Azibo, D. A., 38-39

B

Baer, K. L., 105
Balandier, G.
on the erroneous beliefs of the Congolese about the Europeans, 154
on religious limitations on expansionist activities, 147-148
on violent conflicts in the Congo Kingdom, 145
Barbados, 116
Barker, J. E.
on the Dutch, 8-9
on Dutch history, 24-25
on natural law, 17
Barnet, R. J., 79
Battuta, Ibn, 143
Bellegarde-Smith, Patrick, 86, 117
Benin
living conditions in, 79
Berlin Conference of 1884-1885, 21
Bermuda, 75
Biculturality, 55
Biko, Steve, 59
on overcoming fear of death, 60
on White liberals, 31
Black-on-Black crime and violence, 139
in Africa, 128
in the United States, 101-102
Black Panthers, 53

Black personality, 38
Black Power in South Africa (Gerhart), xiii
Black Skin, White Masks (Fanon), xiii-xiv, xvi-xvii
Black Untouchables, 108-109
Blyden, Edward Wilmot
    on Africa's cooperative spirit, 136
    on collective ownership of land, 148
    on the need for African power, 91
Boers. *See* Afrikaners
Bonaparte, Napoleon, 7-8
Botswana
    life expectancy in, 83
Boukman, Romaine, 153
Brazil
    anti-African practices in, 111-112
    quilombo in, xiii
Britain, V., 79
British Virgin Islands, 75
Brooke, J., 86, 109, 111
Brooks, C. E. P., 149
Brown, L., 104
Bulhan, Hussein A.
    on improving the African condition, 115
    on nonstrugglers' desire for personal survival, 47
    on the opportunistic individual, 53
    on oppression, 49
    on the reactive struggler, 50
    on socialization and personal choice, 39
Burkina Faso
    living conditions in, 79
Burns, J. A., 105

C

Cabral, A.
    on problems, 60
    on the struggle, 39

Index 201

 on struggles for liberation, 125
Cabral, A., xv
 Return to the Source, xvi
Calvinists, 25
Canada
 anti-African practices in, 103-105
 arrest and imprisonment of Blacks in, 104-105
Cape Verde Islands, 140
Capital punishment
 and race, 20
Carthage, 21
Castro, Fidel, 113
Cayman Islands, the, 75
Caesar, Julius
 on Gaul and Germany, 11
Cesaire, Aime
 Discourse on Colonialism, xv
Cesaire, M.
 on White supremacy, 28
Chad, 79
Chimezie, A., 55
Chimusoro, Gideon, 106
China
 anti-African practices in, 106-108
Chinweizu
 on Africa's need for outside assistance, 74
 on delusions of freedom, 45
 on individualism, 47-48
 on opportunistic leaders, 53
 on pride and dignity, 89
 on skin color and oppression, 16
Cholera in Africa, 83
Christianity and White supremacy, 13-15
Cininnatus (Roman Consul), 10
Clarke, John Henrik, 121
 on African people living outside Africa, 119-120

    on the Arab slave trade, 3
    on nationhood and freedom, 18
    Notes For An African World Revolution, 35
    on persecution of early Christians, 15
    on the psychological struggle, 62-63
Climate and Civilization (Huntington), 149
Collingwood, Luke, 19
Colonial rule
    and Africans' adoption of Western cultural values, 125
    Africans' struggles against, 17-18
    effects of, 70-77
    and the partitioning of Africa, 72
    and subsequent dependence on Europeans, 76
Columbia
    anti-African practices in, 110
Communalism, 133-139
    definition of, 135-136
    endurance of, 135
Competitiveness
    absence of among the Lovedu, 129
Conceptual model of orientations, 40-41
Cone, James, 13, 15
Congo
    first Europeans in, 154
    kingdom, 145
Constantine (Roman emperor), 14
Crapanzano, V.
    on European perceptions of Black liberation struggles, 33
    on White fear of retribution from Africans, 29
    on White supremacists, 25
The Crisis of the Negro Intellectual (Cruse), 133
Cruse, Harold
    The Crisis of the Negro Intellectual, 133
Cuba
    anti-African practices in, 113-114
Cultural genocide, xii

Culture
    Black children's preference for White, 41-42
    importance of language to, xi

D

Dagara, the, 137
Dahomey, 78
    boundary dispute with Niger, 146
Davidson, Basil C.
    on Africans' ability to solve problems of survival, 119
    on the Ankole and the Luo, 154
    on antiexpansionist practices in ancient Africa, 145
    on character traits, 132
    on the clannishness of ancient European tribes, 24
    on colonialism, 74
    on colonial rule and indigenous values, 132-133
    on compensation in African judicial practice, 143
    on Dutch settlement at the Cape of Good Hope, 25
    on the effects of European civilization on Africa, 71
    on Russian expectation for Africa, 106
    on the Shona, 152-153
    on trade with Europe, 78
    on traditional African thought on qualities of ideal people, 129
    on tribalism, 72
    on unity of Whites against non-Whites, 25
Debt of African states, 87-89
Decolonizing the Mind (Wa Thiong'o), xii
Deforestation in Africa, 81
Delafosse, M., 147
Deracinated Black elite, 57
Desertification of Africa, 148
The Destruction of Black Civilization (Williams), 1
De Villiers, M.
    on Afrikaners' beliefs about political superiority, 22
    on segregation, 27

DeWitt, K., 110
Diop, Cheikh Anta
    on African disunity, 121
    on antiexpansionist tendencies of ancient Egyptians, 147
    on the autonomy of the nomadic life, 23-24
    on European self-reliance, 7
    on Europeans' environment and materialism, 6-7
    on infanticide in ancient Sparta, 10
    on moral differences between Egyptians and Eurasians, 143
Discourse on Colonialism (Cesaire), xv
Dominican Republic, 117-118
Double consciousness, 55
Dravidians, 108
Du Bois, W. E. B.
    on communism of industry, 136
    on the degradation of Africa, 70-71
    on double consciousness, 55
    on mechanical power making Europe ruler of the world, 4
    on the position of women in ancient Africa, 130
    on replacement of African goods with European, 69
    on the slave trade and African development, 69
Dutch East India Company, 22

E

Ecological crisis in Africa, 148-149
Egypt
    antiexpansionist tendencies in ancient, 147
    knowledge of gunpowder in ancient, 141
    Sabacos rule of, 23
    use of iron in ancient, 141-142
Enslavement
    of Africans
        and African adoption of Western cultural values, 125
        by Arabs, 3
        by the British, 19
        as cause of White xenophobia, 26

Index

as contributing factor in African disunity, 70
by the Dutch, 37
by the Portuguese, 69
of Whites, 16
Environmental degradation of Africa, 148-152
Environmental racism, 85-87
Ethiopia
    ancient, 146
    defeat of Mussolini in, 17
    environmental degradation of war in, 148-149
    Italian occupation of, 21
    kinship as factor in victory over Italians, 139-140
    life expectancy in, 83
Euclid, 67
Eurocentric curriculum, x
Europeans
    acquisitiveness of, 19
    Africans as property of, 18-19
    anti-African practices of, 93-95
    cultural symbols of, 11-12
    early, 6-7, 18
    exploitive trade with Africa, 69
    expropriation of African lands by, 21-23
    and isolation of African powers, 18
    psychohistorical traditions of, 12-13
    psychology of, 6-13
    sacredness of life to, 20
    traditional values of, 138-139
Evans-Pritchard, E. E., 135

F
Fanon, Frantz
    Black Skin, White Masks, xiii-xiv, xvi-xvii
    on conversion of the oppressor, 56
    on existing, 59
    on nonstrugglers, 45, 47

  on opportunistic individuals, 52
  on self-empowerment, 51
  on violence and aggressiveness of Whites, 16
  Wretched of the Earth, 1
Farnsworth, C. H., 104-105
Food crisis in Africa, 79-83
  external factors in, 82
Foreign aid
  in Mozambique, 80
Fortes, M., 135
Fredrickson, George
  on abolition of slavery in United States, 26
Freire, Paulo
  on authentic strugglers, 61
  on the development of the oppressed, 58
  on nonstrugglers, 45, 46
  on the quest for White approval, 56
French Guiana, 75
Fromm, Erich, 45
Fuller, N., 46

G
Galla, the, 145
Garson, P., 141
Garvey, Marcus, 59, 121
  on his desire for Africa's redemption, 60
  on instruction of children, 42
  on the need for Black independence, 65
Gerhart, Gail M.
  Black Power in South Africa, xiii
Germany
  anti-African practices in, 94-95
  reunification of, 11
Ghana, 17
  living conditions in, 79
Gibson, Richard, 75, 140

God
    blaming the difficulties of Blacks on, 45-46
    life as gift of, 142-143, 150
    natural environment as a gift of, 150
    traditional African beliefs about, 128
Gold, Herbert, 117
Goodman, W., 46
Gratian (Roman emperor), 14
Great Britain
    anti-African practices in, 95-98
    arrest and imprisonment of Blacks in, 97
    unemployment and underemployment of Blacks in, 97-98
Greenberg, J., 20
Grenada, 116
Guadeloupe, 75
Guinea, 140
Guinea-Bissau
    life expectancy in, 83
Gyeke, Kwame
    on Africans' worshipful attitude toward nature, 150
    on Akan moral thought, 129
    on communalism, 135-136
    on traditional African concepts, 138

H

Hacker, Andrew, 99, 102
Hadjor, K. B., 72, 74
Haiti
    anti-African practices in, 116-118
    life expectancy in, 83
    revolution against the French, 17, 153
Hama, B., 142
Hampate Ba, A., 128
    on African mythology, 151
Haq, F., 106
Hasenbalg, C. A., 111

Herodotus
   on antiexpansionistic tendencies in ancient Africa, 147
   on barbarians, 10
   on death penalty in Nubia, 143
Herroros, the, 72
Herskovits, Melville J.
   on ancient Africans' use of tools, 141
   on migration and the ice age, 149
   on the Sahara during the Quatenary period, 150
Hertz, F.
   on ancient conquest, 8
   on characteristics of Gauls and Germans, 11
   on the Roman punishment for theft, 145
   on the scarcity of metal ores in the Nile Valley, 142
Hevi, J. E., 107
Hiernaux, J., 150
Higginbotham, Leon, 102-103
Hoare, P., 19
Holocaust, the, 28
Homicide against African-Americans, 20
Hord, Fred Lee
   Reconstructing Memory, xii
Horsman, R., 98
Hountondji, Paulin, 126
Huntington, Ellsworth
   Climate and Civilization, 149
Hutchinson, A., 107
Hyksos, the, 3, 68, 147

I

Iliffe, J., 135
Independence
   Africans' struggles for, 17-18
India
   anti-African practices in, 108-109
Inkatha, 140

Intermarriage between races, 25
   in China, 107
   in Cuba, 113
   in Latin America, 114
   in Venezuela, 113
International Monetary Fund (IMF), 88, 89
Iron
   in ancient Egypt, 141-142
   discovery of by Africans, 141
Italy
   colonial rule over Ethiopia, 139-140
   proposal to dispose of toxic waste from, 86

J
Jaarsveld, Adriaan van, 22
Jackson, J. C., 142
Jagas of Matamba, the, 140
Jamaica, 17
   debt crisis in, 88
   unemployment rate of Blacks in, 116
Jean, C. M., 133, 156
Jinga (Nzingha) (Angolan queen), 140
Johnson, D., 53
Jujun, the, 146
Justinian I (Roman emperor), 15

K
Kalabari, the, 152
Kelso, B. J., 76
Kennedy, Paul
   on war and the European powers, 32-33
   on wars between European states, 10
   on White supremacy, 4
Kenya
   the Luo of, 154
   Mau Mau fighters, 17

Khopa, B., 128
Kinship. See Communalism
Ki-Zerbo, J., 142, 149
Kock, V. J. (Rhodesian magistrate), 20
Kodjo, Edem
    on African production of manufactured goods, 85
    on early African society, 77
    on Eurocentric control of the world, 21
    on gun supply, 17
    on lack of African defense policies, 18
Kovel, J., 30-31
Krige, E. J.
    on Lovedu of the Transvaal and nature, 151
    on the moral code of the Lovedu, 128-129
    on restitutive sanctions, 137
Krige, J. D.
    on Lovedu of the Transvaal and nature, 151
    on the moral code of the Lovedu, 128-129
    on restitutive sanctions, 137
Kung, the, 144

L
Land
    collective ownership of, 147-148
Language
    importance of to culture, xi
Latin America
    anti-African practices in, 109-118
    miscegenation in, 114
Leakey, Louis S. B., 126
    on death penalty among Bantus, 143
    on drunkenness, 101
    on the position of women in ancient Africa, 130
Lethoso
    life expectancy in, 83
Levitt, K. P., 88

Index

Lewis, B., 3, 30
Liberia, 21
    attempts by to annex part of Sierra Leone, 146
Life expectancy of Blacks
    in Africa, 83
    in Brazil, 111
    in Haiti, 83
    in Harlem, 83
    in Sierra Leone, 83
Livy (Roman historian), 11
L'Ouverture, Toussaint, 59
Lovedu of the Transvaal
    moral code of, 128-129
    religious beliefs of, 151
Lugard, Lady
    on the achievements of Africans, 155
    on northern European nomads, 11
Lumumba, Patrice, 59
    on the Congo, 60
Luo, the, 154
Lying
    traditional African beliefs on, 128, 129
Lynch, H. R., 136
    on cultural nationalism, 125

M

Ma'at, 141
Madhubuti, Haki R., x
Malawi
    boundary dispute with Tanzania, 146
    living conditions in, 79
Malcolm X, 59
Mali, 77
    infant mortality in, 84
    justice in, 143
    living conditions in, 79

Manelukes
    revolt of, 16
Manichean world, 39
    Black children unprepared for a, 42
    nonstrugglers in, 47
Maquet, J. J., 138
Maroons (Jamaican slaves), 17
Martinique, 75
Mathabane, M., 56
Mazrui, Ali
    on Africans' oneness with nature, 150
    on animism, 152
    on the restoration of ecological balance in Africa, 149
McCain, P., 103, 105
Meldrum, A., 76
Memmi, A.
    on individual solutions to collective problems, 54
    on the partially committed struggler, 54-55
    on the power of the colonizer, 58
    success in the Manichean world, 47
Military armaments, 17, 75
        spending on, 127
Mind of South Africa (Sparks), 138
Miscegenation. See Intermarriage between races
The Miseducation of the Negro (Woodson), x
Monotheism, 67
Moore-King, Bruce
    on the power of groups, 31
    on Zimbabwe after independence, 138
    on Zimbabwean war of independence, 13, 28-29
Motley, J. L., 8, 11
Mozambique, 17, 140
    Black soldiers in Portuguese army in, 75
    environmental degradation of war in, 148-149
    food crisis in, 80
    living conditions in, 79

Index

Mphahlele, E., 131
Mugabe, Robert, 76
Museveni, Yoweri, 120
Mussolini, Benito, 17

N

Namibia, 72, 140
    attempts at racial reconciliation in, 76
Nash, N., 109-110
National Union for the Total Independence of Angola (UNITA), 80
National Urban League, 103
Native Land Acts of 1913 (South Africa), 26
Nazimpaka Yubi III of Rwanda, 154-155
Nehru, Jawaharial, 11-12, 108
Netherlands, the
    history of, 24
Netherlands Antilles, 75
Ngola, the, 140
Ngugi Wa Thiong'o. *See* Wa Thiong'o, Ngugi
Niebuhr, Reinhold, 23
Niger
    boundary dispute with Dahomey, 146
    living conditions in, 79
Nigeria, 146
Nile Valley
    history of, 134
    metal ores in, 142
Nkrumah, Kwame, 121
Nobles, W. W., 48
Nonstrugglers, 44-48
    desire for personal survival, 47
    failure to confront oppression, 47
    receptiveness of, 45
    victim-focused identity of, 46
Notes for an African World Revolution (Clarke), 35

Nubia
 antiexpansionist past of, 147
 death penalty in ancient, 143
Nuers, the, 144
Nyakusa, the, 144
Nyakyusa of Tanzania, the, 132
Nyerere, Julius
 on African economic development, 73
Nzingha, Queen of Angola, 59, 140

O
Of Water and the Spirit (Some'), 137
Oguntoye, K., 94
Onyango Dunde, 154
Opitz, M., 94
Opportunistic individuals, 51-54
 and appearance of commitment, 51
 deficiencies of, 51-52
 as problems to the African community, 53
 shortcomings of as leaders, 53-54
Oppression of Africans
 reasons for, 16-17
Organization of African Unity (OAU), 73
Orphans, 84, 130-131
Osie Tutu, 153
Ostheimer, J. M.
 on lack of inter-African coordination, 73
 on safeguarding refugees, 81

P
Pan-Africanism, 121-122
 need for Africans to internalize, 139
 rejection of by postcolonial African leaders, 73
Panama
 anti-African practices in, 110-111
Park, Mungo, 130, 152

Index 215

Partially committed strugglers, 54-58
    as approximation to the ideal orientation, 54
    double consciousness in, 55
    transformation to totally committed, 56-57
Peru
    anti-African practices in, 109
Plato, 67
Plotinus (ancient Egyptian), 14
Plumpp, Sterling, 55
Pondo of South Eastern Africa, the, 132
Psychology of dependency, 70

R
Racial socialization, 41-43
Rajshekar, V. T., 108-109
Reactive strugglers, 48-51
    control of by the oppressor, 49
    as part of a collective effort, 48
    self-empowerment for, 51
Reconstructing Memory (Hord), xii
Refugees, 127
    from Mozambique, 80
    problems of, 81
Return to the Source (Cabral), xvi
Robertson, Robert, 105
Rodney, W.
    on education in Africa, 85
    on imposition of European cultural standards, 70
    on the slave trade and socioeconomic development, 69
Rogers, J. A., 105
Rose, J. H., 7-8
Rout, L., 109, 110, 111
Rowlands, Basil, 20
Russia
    anti-African practices in, 105-106

S

Sabacos (ancient Ethiopian), 23
Sahara Desert
    in the Quatenary period, 150
St. Kitts, 116
St. Lucia, 116
Sartre, J. P., 49
Sautman, B., 107, 108
Schultz, D., 94
Seegers, A., 75
Segregation
    primordial tendency of Europeans toward, 23-27
    in South Africa, 26
    in the United States, 26
Semaj, L. T.
    on Eurocentric and Afrocentric worldviews, 38
    on partially committed individuals, 55
Shona, the, 152-153
Sierra Leone
    attempts by Liberia to annex parts of, 146
    life expectancy in, 83
Simmons, M., 93
Skin color as a stimulus for tyranny, 3, 16, 40
Slavery and the slave trade. *See* Enslavement of Africans
Smith, E., 153
Smith, J. H., 14
Snowden, F., 146
Snyder, C. P., 75
Social and socioeconomic stratification
    absence of among the Lovedu, 129
    in contemporary Africa, 132
Social Darwinism, 25
Socialism
    in African Society, 136
Socialization of White youth, 43
Sokee, Chief of the Niger, 152

Somalia
    environmental degradation of war in, 148-149
    living conditions in, 79
Some', Malidoma
Of Water and the Spirit, 137
South Africa, 74. *See also* Afrikaners
    Black Consciousness Movement in, xiii
    Black disunity in, 140-141
    expropriation of by Europeans, 22
South America
    anti-African practices in, 109-110, 111-113
South West Africa People's Organization (Swapo), 76
Sparks, Allister
    on conflict among Afrikaners, 25
    on illness in less developed countries in Africa, 83
    The Mind of South Africa, 138
    on nonstrugglers, 44
    on psychological effects of enslavement, 37
Spencer, M. B.
    on African-American child-rearing practices, 42
Steele, Shelby
    on Blacks with a victim-focused identity, 46
Stereotypes of Blacks
    in China, 107
    in Columbia, 110
    in Russia, 105
    sexual, 107, 118
    in the United States, 102
Stuckey, S., 42

T
Tallensi, the, 144, 145
Tanzania
    boundary dispute with Malawi, 146
Tempels, Placide, 142, 151
Terkel, S., 103

Theft
    mitigating circumstances for, 145
Theodosius I (Roman emperor), 14-15
Thiong'o, Ngugi Wa. *See* Wa Thiong'o, Ngugi
Thom, W. G., 73
Thompson, L., 25
Timberlake, L., 81
Tivs, the, 146
Tobago, 116
Toxic waste, 85-87
    Italian, 86
    in the United States, 86-87
    World Bank on, 86
Tribalism, 72
Trinidad, 116
Trotha, Lothar von, 72
Trujillo, Rafael, 117
Tswana, the, 136-137
Tucker, F. H., 11
Turok, L., 88

U

Unemployment and underemployment of Blacks
    in Brazil, 112
    in Caribbean nations, 116
    in England, 97-98
    in St. Croix, 116
United States
    anti-African practices in, 98-103
    arrest and imprisonment of Blacks in, 100-102
    environmental racism in, 86-87
    medical care of Blacks in, 100
    mortgage discrimination against Blacks in, 100
    poverty of Blacks in, 99
    unemployment and underemployment of Blacks in, 99-100
Uruguay

anti-African practices in, 109-110

V
Vandals, 21
Van Sertima, Ivan, 67, 141
Venezuela
    anti-African practices in, 112-113
Vercoutter, J., 134
Violence
    Black-on-Black, 101-102, 128, 139
    traditional views of, 141-146
Vlahos, O., 130, 144-145

W
War
    cost of, 143-146
    humaneness of in ancient Africa, 144-146
    traditional African views of, 141-146
Wa Thiong'o, Ngugi, xi, xv
    Decolonizing the Mind, xii
    on struggle, xvi
Welsing, Frances Cress, 26-27
White supremacy
    and the African world, 16-18
    decline in after World War II, 28
    definition of, 5
    origins of, 4-5
    perpetuation of by South Afrikaner Boers, 9
    and religion, 13-15
    and White liberals, 31-32
    Whites' response to, 28
Williams, Chancellor
    on African history, 37
    on Africans who did not submit, 60
    The Destruction of Black Civilization, 1
    on humaneness of war in ancient Africa, 144

on revolt of the Manelukes, 16
on White supremacists, 9
Williams, H. Sylvester, 121
Wilson, Amos
    on Black-on-Black violence, 101
Wiredu, J. E., 127
Women
    position of in ancient Africa, 130
Woods, F., 15
Woodson, Carter G., x, 15
    on the ideal struggler, 58-59
    The Miseducation of the Negro, x
World Bank
    and Africa's debt crisis, 87-89
    as representative of Western capitalist interests, 89
    on toxic waste, 86
Wretched of the Earth (Fanon), 1
Wright, Bobby, 31, 45
Wright, W. R., 112-113

X
Xhosa, 21
    enslavement of by the Dutch, 37

Y
Yuan, Gao, 106-107

Z
Zaire
    living conditions in, 79
Zimbabwe, 17, 140
    after independence, 138
    influence of White minority in, 76
    war of independence, 13
    White Rhodesian soldiers in, 28-29
Zong (British slave ship), 19